daybook, *n.* a book in which the events of the day are recorded; *specif.* a journal or diary

DAYBOOK
of Critical Reading and Writing

AUTHOR

VICKI SPANDEL

CONSULTING AUTHORS

RUTH NATHAN

LAURA ROBB

Great Source Education Group
a Houghton Mifflin Company
Wilmington, Massachusetts

AUTHOR

VICKI SPANDEL, director of Write Traits, provides training to writing teachers both nationally and internationally. A former teacher and journalist, Vicki is author of more than twenty books, including the new third edition of **Creating Writers.**

CONSULTING AUTHORS

RUTH NATHAN, one of the authors of **Writers Express** and **Write Away,** is the author of many professional books and articles on literacy. She currently teaches in third grade as well as consults with numerous schools and organizations on reading.

LAURA ROBB, author of **Reading Strategies That Work** and **Teaching Reading in Middle School,** has taught language arts at Powhatan School in Boyce, Virginia, for more than thirty years. She also mentors and coaches teachers in Virginia public schools and speaks at conferences throughout the country.

Printed in the United States of America

International Standard Book Number: 0-669-48038-X

2 3 4 5 6 7 8 9 10 - BA - 06 05 04 03 02 01

3

4

5

6

Active Reading

Do you have friends who are always on the move? Active readers are always doing something too. They predict, question, and visualize. Active readers mark up the text by circling, highlighting, underlining, and taking notes.

This Daybook will help you become a more active reader. You'll learn and practice different strategies for getting involved with your reading. And, when you get involved by reading actively, you'll find you understand and remember more of what you read.

ACTIVE READING · Mark Up the Text

Active readers mark up the text when they come across important ideas or other things they want to remember. Then, if they need to look back at what they read, their eyes will automatically go to the marked-up parts. To mark up, you might highlight, underline, circle, or star. (Remember: only mark up your own books, not books belonging to the school or library.) Here's how one reader marked up the following passage from "The Three-Century Woman" by Richard Peck.

Response Notes

Example:

Hah hah. Pretty funny.

* Wow! That's a long time!

I wonder why she doesn't want her to be interviewed?

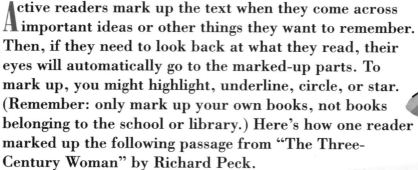

The Three-Century Woman by Richard Peck

"I guess if you live long enough," my mom said to Aunt Gloria, "you get your fifteen minutes of fame."

Mom was on the car phone to Aunt Gloria. The minute Mom rolls out of the garage, she's on her car phone. It's state of the art and better than her car.

We were heading for Whispering Oaks to see my Great-Grandmother Breckenridge, who's lived there since I was a little girl. They call it an Elder Care Facility. Needless to say, I hated going.

The reason for Great-Grandma's fame is that she was born in 1899. Now it's January 2001. If you're one of those people who claim the new century begins in 2001, not 2000, even you have to agree that Great-Grandma Breckenridge has lived in three centuries. This is her claim to fame.

We waited for a light to change along by Northbrook Mall, and I gazed fondly over at it. Except for the Multiplex, it was closed because of New Year's Day. I have a severe mall habit. But I'm fourteen, and the mall is the place without homework. Aunt Gloria's voice filled the car.

"If you take my advice," she told Mom, "you'll keep those Whispering Oaks people from letting the media in to interview Grandma. Interview her my foot! Honestly. She doesn't even know where she is, let alone how many centuries she's lived in. The poor old soul. Leave her in peace. She's already got one foot in the—"

8

ACTIVE READING Predict

Active readers **predict** what's going to happen before they read and while they are reading. It helps them get involved in the story. Here are one reader's predictions for the next part of "The Three-Century Woman." To make predictions, use what you already know and clues from the story in order to figure out what will happen next.

The Three-Century Woman by Richard Peck

"Gloria, your trouble is you have no sense of history." Mom gunned across the intersection. "You got a C in History."

"I was sick a lot that year," Aunt Gloria said.

"Sick of history," Mom murmured.

"I heard that," Aunt Gloria said.

They bickered on, but I tuned them out. Then when we turned in at Whispering Pines, a sound truck from IBC-TV was blocking the drive.

"Good grief," Mom murmured. "TV."

"I told you," Aunt Gloria said, but Mom switched her off. She parked in a frozen rut.

"I'll wait in the car," I said. "I have homework."

"Get out of the car," Mom said.

If you get so old you have to be put away, Whispering Oaks isn't that bad. It smells all right, and a Christmas tree glittered in the lobby. A real tree. On the other hand, you have to push a red button to unlock the front door. I guess it's to keep the inmates from escaping, though Great-Grandma Breckenridge wasn't going anywhere and hadn't for twenty years.

When we got to her wing, the hall was full of camera crews and a woman from the suburban newspaper with a notepad.

Mom sighed. It was like that first day of school when you think you'll be okay until the teachers learn your name. Stepping over a cable, we stopped at Great-Grandma's door, and they were on to us.

Response Notes

I bet the T.V. truck is there to interview Great-Grandma.

I predict they won't be allowed to do the interview.

9

A ctive readers also ask questions when they're reading. Do you sometimes ask questions about things you don't understand, like unfamiliar words or ideas? Do you ever question why a character does something or how a story turns out? Here's how one reader asked questions while reading the next part of "The Three-Century Woman."

Response Notes

Is that a kind of sickness?

10

The Three-Century Woman by Richard Peck

"Who are you people to Mrs. Breckenridge?" the newspaperwoman said. "I want names."

These people were seriously pushy. And the TV guy was wearing more makeup than Mom. It dawned on me that they couldn't get into Great-Grandma's room without her permission. Mom turned on them.

"Listen, you're not going to be interviewing my grandmother," she said in a quiet bark. "I'll be glad to tell you anything you want to know about her, but you're not going in there. She's got nothing to say, and . . . she needs a lot of rest."

"Is it Alzheimer's?" the newswoman asked. "Because we're thinking Alzheimer's."

"Think what you want," Mom said. "But this is as far as you get. And you people with the camera and the light, you're not going in there either. You'd scare her to death, and then I'd sue the pants off you."

They pulled back.

But a voice came wavering out of Great-Grandma's room. Quite an eerie, echoing voice.

"Let them in!" the voice said.

It had to be Great-Grandma Breckenridge. Her roommate had died. "Good grief," Mom murmured, and the press surged forward.

Mom and I went in first, and our eyes popped. Great-Grandma was usually flat out in the bed, dozing, with her teeth in a glass and a book in her hand. Today she was bright-eyed and propped up. She wore a fuzzy pink bed jacket. A matching bow was stuck in what remained of her hair.

ACTIVE READING Visualize

Active readers **visualize,** or create pictures in their heads as they read. Visualizing helps readers "see" a selection. When you visualize, you might want to draw a simple sketch or drawing. Here's what one reader "saw" while reading the next part of "The Three-Century Woman."

Response Notes

The Three-Century Woman by Richard Peck

"Oh for pity's sake," Mom murmured. "They've got her done up like a Barbie doll."

Great-Grandma peered from the bed at Mom. "And who are you?" she asked.

"I'm Ann," Mom said carefully. "This is Megan," she said, meaning me.

"That's right," Great-Grandma said. "At least you know who you are. Plenty around this place don't."

The guy with the camera on his shoulder barged in. The other guy turned on a blinding light.

Great-Grandma blinked. In the glare we noticed she wore a trace of lipstick. <u>The TV anchor elbowed the woman reporter aside and stuck a mike in Great-Grandma's face.</u> Her claw hand came out from under the covers and tapped it.

"Is this thing on?" she inquired.

"Yes, ma'am," the TV anchor said in his broadcasting voice. "Don't you worry about all this modern technology. We don't understand half of it ourselves." He gave her his big, five-thirty news smile and settled on the edge of her bed. There was room for him. She was tiny.

"We're here to congratulate you for having lived in three centuries—for being a Three-Century Woman! A great achievement."

Great-Grandma waved a casual claw. "Nothing to it," she said. "You sure this mike's on? Let's do this in one take."

The cameraman snorted and moved in for a closer shot. Mom stood still as a statue, wondering what was going to come out of Great-Grandma's mouth next.

As you read this Daybook, try to mark up the text, predict, question, and visualize. Write in the Response Notes space beside each selection. Look back at the examples if you need help. Practice as you continue reading "The Three-Century Woman." Try to use at least two of the strategies as you finish the story.

Response Notes

must have been scary.

12

The Three-Century Woman by Richard Peck

"Mrs. Breckenridge," the anchor said, "to what do you attribute your long life?"

"I was only married once," Great-Grandma said. "And he died young."

The anchor stared. "Ah. And anything else?"

"Yes. I don't look back. I live in the present."

The camera panned around the room. This was all the present she had, and it didn't look like much.

"You live for the present," the anchor said, looking for an angle, "even now?"

Great-Grandma nodded. "Something's always happening. Last night I fell off the bed pan."

Mom groaned.

The cameraman pulled in for a tighter shot. The anchor seemed to search his mind. You could tell he thought he was a great interviewer, though he had no sense of humor. A tiny smile played around Great-Grandma's wrinkled lips.

"But you've lived through amazing times, Mrs. Breckenridge. And you never think back about them?"

Great-Grandma stroked her chin and considered. "You mean you want to hear something interesting? Like how I lived through the San Francisco earthquake—the big one of oh-six?"

Beside me, Mom stirred. We were crowded over by the dead lady's bed. "You survived the 1906 San Francisco earthquake?" the anchor said.

The Three-Century Woman by Richard Peck

Great-Grandma gazed at the ceiling, lost in thought.

"I'd have been about seven years old. My folks and I were staying at that big hotel. You know the one. I slept in a cot at the foot of their bed. In the middle of the night, that room gave a shake, and the chiffonier walked right across the floor. You know what chiffonier is?"

"A chest of drawers?" the anchor said.

"Close enough," Great-Grandma said. "And the pictures flapped on the walls. We had to walk down twelve flights because the elevators didn't work. When we got outside, the streets were ankle-deep in broken glass. You never saw such a mess in your life."

Mom nudged me and hissed: "She's never been to San Francisco. She's never been west of Denver. I've heard her say so."

"Incredible!" the anchor said.

"Truth's stranger than fiction," Great-Grandma said, smoothing her sheet.

"And you never think back about it?"

Great-Grandma shrugged her little fuzzy pink shoulders. "I've been through too much. I don't have time to remember it all. I was on the Hindenburg when it blew up, you know."

Mom moaned, and the cameraman was practically standing on his head for a close-up.

"The Hindenburg?"

"That big gas bag the Germans built to fly over the Atlantic Ocean. It was called a zeppelin. Biggest thing you ever saw—five city blocks long. It was in May of 1937, before your time. You wouldn't remember. My husband and I were coming back from Europe on it. No, wait a minute."

Great-Grandma cocked her head and pondered for the camera.

what is that

The Three-Century Woman by Richard Peck

"My husband was dead by then. It was some other man. Anyway, the two of us were coming back on the Hindenburg. It was smooth as silk. You didn't know you were moving. When we flew in over New York, they stopped the ball game at Yankee Stadium to see us passing overhead."

Great-Grandma paused, caught up in memories.

"And then the Hindenburg exploded," the anchor said, prompting her.

She nodded. "We had no complaints about the trip till then. The luggage was all stacked, and we were coming in at Lakehurst, New Jersey. I was wearing my beige coat—beige or off-white, I forget. Then whoosh! The gondola heated up like an oven, and people peeled out of the windows. We hit the ground and bounced. When we hit again, the door fell off, and I walked out and kept going. When they caught up with me in the parking lot, they wanted to put me in the hospital. I looked down and thought I was wearing a lace dress. The fire had about burned up my coat. And I lost a shoe."

"Fantastic!" the anchor breathed. "What detail!" Behind him the woman reporter was scribbling away on her pad.

"Never," Mom muttered. "Never in her life."

"Ma'am, you are living history!" the anchor said. "In your sensational span of years you've

The Three-Century Woman by Richard Peck

survived two great disasters!"

"Three." Great-Grandma patted the bow on her head. "I told you I'd been married."

"And before we leave this (venerable) lady," the anchor said, flashing a smile for the camera, "we'll ask Mrs. Breckenridge if she has any predictions for this new twenty-first century ahead of us here in the Dawn of the Millennium."

"Three or four predictions," Great-Grandma said, and paused again, stretching out her airtime. "Number one, taxes will be higher. Number two, it's going to be harder to find a place to park. And number three, a whole lot of people are going to live as long as I have, so get ready for us."

"And with those wise words," the anchor said, easing off the bed, "we leave Mrs. Breck—"

"And one more prediction," she said. "TV's on the way out. Your network ratings are already in the basement. It's all websites now. Son, I predict you'll be looking for work."

And that was it. The light went dead. The anchor, looking shaken, followed his crew out the door. When TV's done with you, they're done with you. "Is that a wrap?" Great-Grandma asked.

But now the woman from the suburban paper was moving in on her. "Just a few more questions, Mrs. Breckenridge.

"Where you from?" Great-Grandma blinked pinkeyed at her.

"The Glenview Weekly Shopper."

"You bring a still photographer with you?" Great-Grandma asked.

"Well, no."

"And you never learned shorthand either, did you?"

"Well . . . no."

"Honey, I only deal with professionals. There's the door."

15

The Three-Century Woman by Richard Peck

So then it was just Mom and Great-Grandma and I in the room. Mom planted a hand on her hip. "Grandma. Number one, you've never been to San Francisco. And number two, you never *saw* one of those zeppelin things."

Great-Grandma shrugged. "No, but I can read." She nodded to the pile of books on her nightstand with her spectacles folded on top. "You can pick up all that stuff in books."

"And number three," Mom said. "Your husband didn't die young. I can *remember* Grandpa Breckenridge."

"It was that TV dude in the five-hundred-dollar suit who set me off," Great-Grandma said. "He dyes his hair, did you notice? He made me mad, and it put my nose out of joint. He didn't notice I'm still here. He thought I was nothing but my memories. So I gave him some."

Now Mom and I stood beside her bed.

"I'll tell you something else," Great-Grandma said. "And it's no lie."

We waited, holding our breath to hear. Great-Grandma Breckenridge was pointing her little old bent finger right at me. "You, Megan," she said. "Once upon a time, I was your age. How scary is that?"

Then she hunched up her little pink shoulders and winked at me. She grinned and I grinned. She was just this little withered-up leaf of a lady in the bed. But I felt like giving her a kiss on her little wrinkled cheek, so I did.

"I'll come to see you more often," I told her.

"Call first," she said. "I might be busy." Then she dozed.

Reading Well

Most people enjoy things they're good at, whether it's playing a sport, mastering a computer game—or reading. Good readers are active readers, which means they get involved in what they read. In this Daybook, you'll respond to what you read in a variety of ways. This Daybook will show you ways not only to enjoy reading, but also get more out of it.

In the first unit, you'll get involved by asking questions, highlighting, forming pictures in your mind, and pausing to check your understanding. You'll practice the reading skills of predicting, making inferences, identifying the main idea, and reflecting. So go ahead—start on the path to becoming a more active reader.

Thinking Ahead

When you get caught up in reading a story, do you ever get hunches about what will happen next? If you do, you're practicing one of the skills of an active reader. When you **predict, you use what you already know to guess what will happen next.** Making predictions increases your involvement in a story. It makes you want to read on to find out if your hunches are correct.

As you read the following Native American folktale, stop each time you see the "Stop and Predict" sign. Then ask yourself: "What do I think will happen next?" Write your prediction in the Response Notes.

Response Notes

18

Example:

I predict that Little Hare will be in trouble if he bothers Flying Ant.

Little Hare and the Pine Tree
by Joseph Bruchac

A WINNEBAGO STORY

One day, as Little Hare was out running all around the earth, he saw a great monster coming towards him. It was Flying Ant. Flying Ant had a huge body, but his rawhide belt was bound so tight about him that his waist was very small. Flying Ant had pulled up a great spruce tree and was using it as a club. As he walked around and walked around the hills he pounded his club on the ground and sang his hunting song. Whenever he saw an animal of some kind, he would throw the tree at it, crushing the animal with its roots. Then he would pick that animal up and swallow it.

As Flying Ant came striding over the hills towards him, Little Hare laughed.

"Hey," Little Hare said, "his waist is as thin as a hair. I will blow him in two." Then Little Hare began to blow. *"Whooo, whooo."*

STOP and Predict

Flying Ant paid no attention. He threw his spruce tree club and it flattened Little Hare.

But when Flying Ant lifted up the tree, he was not pleased at what he found.

© GREAT SOURCE. COPYING IS PROHIBITED.

Little Hare and the Pine Tree
by Joseph Bruchac

"Hungh," Flying Ant said, picking the little thing up by its ears and then throwing it away, "this is no good to eat."

When Little Hare did not come home that night, his grandmother became worried. Little Hare always came home at night, even though he ran all over the earth each day. "My grandson has been killed," she said.

When morning came, Grandmother tied her dress up above her knees and went out to look for Little Hare. She ran all over the earth looking. Then she heard the sound of Flying Ant pounding his club and singing his hunting song.

As soon as Flying Ant saw Grandmother, he lifted his club to throw it.

"Brother," Grandmother said, "you should not do that."

Immediately Flying Ant lowered his club.

"Old Woman," Flying Ant said, "I did not recognize you. What do you want?"

"I am afraid my grandson has been killed. I think perhaps he bothered you and you killed him."

"What kind of a grandson was it? Was it a big tasty one good to eat or a little smelly one not big enough to keep?"

"A little one, Brother."

"It may be that I did kill him," Flying Ant said. "Yesterday I killed something very little that was no good to eat. I threw it away down there in the swamp."

Grandmother went down into the swamp. There was Little Hare, flattened out and dead. She grabbed him by the ears and shook him.

"Grandson," she said in a stern voice, "you have slept too long. It is time to wake up and work."

As soon as she dropped him back on the ground he jumped up, ran in a circle and then sat there.

Little Hare and the Pine Tree
by Joseph Bruchac

"Grandmother," he said, "I was sleeping soundly. Why did you wake me up?"

"You were not asleep," Grandmother said. "The big Old One who walks and walks around the hills killed you. You bothered him yesterday. I made you alive again."

"You are right," Little Hare said. "I remember now. Tomorrow I will go and see him again."

Then Little Hare went home with his grandmother. He ate and ate, and when the morning came he ate again. Then he was ready to set out. He ran all over the world until he came to the end of the earth. There the tall pine trees grew. Little Hare went to the tallest of all the pines. He ran around the tree four times and then he placed tobacco at its base.

"Pine Tree," he said, "I wish to use you. Allow me to pull you from the ground. I need you to help me. There is a big Old One who crushes all the plants and animals. I will set you back here again when I am done."

STOP and Predict

Little Hare grabbed hold of the great pine. As soon as he did so, he began to grow until he was the same height as the big tree. He pulled and the big pine came out easily by its roots. Then Little Hare went back to the hills where Flying Ant walked around and walked around. When Flying Ant saw Little Hare he began to pound his club on the ground and sing his song. Little Hare did the same and they danced towards each other, singing and pounding the earth. But Little Hare danced faster than Flying Ant. The earth shook as Little Hare pounded it with the great pine tree. As Little

20

a tall tale

Little Hare and the Pine Tree
By Joseph Bruchac

Response Notes

Hare danced closer and closer, Flying Ant became afraid. He lifted up his club and shouted, but Little Hare was too quick for him. Little Hare lifted the great pine up and struck the monster. His blow was so strong that it broke Flying Ant into many pieces. Each piece became a winged ant and flew away.

"So it will be from now on," Little Hare said. "No longer will ants be huge monsters. They will always be small."

And so it has been to this day.

Then Little Hare carried the great pine tree back to the place where it had been growing.

"Thank you, Pine Tree," Little Hare said.

Then he set it back carefully into the earth. And if you do not believe my story, just go to that hill. You will see that tree. It still grows there to this day.

21

How well did your predictions match what actually happened? Tell what information in the story you used to make each of your predictions.

First prediction:

Information used from story:

Second prediction:

Information used from story:

⊶ The author ends this tale with Flying Ant breaking into millions of small pieces. What is another way to end the story? Your predictions might help you come up with an idea.

New Ending:

As you read, ask yourself: "What do I think will happen next?"

Reading Between the Lines

An **inference** is a reasonable guess based on information in the story. Here's an example. An author describes a character stomping her feet and yelling. One reasonable inference you could make from this is that the character is angry.

Read the passage from *Princess in the Pigpen*. See what inferences you can make about the main character, Elizabeth, and her situation. As you read, highlight clues about who the girl is and where she comes from. In the Response Notes, jot down the inferences you make.

from *Princess in the Pigpen*
by Jane Resh Thomas

A narrow shaft of sunlight shimmered in the crack between the curtains, fell across the darkened bed, and struck Elizabeth's face. The glare in the gloom stunned her eyes and hurt her pounding head.

In the next instant, Elizabeth heard a noise like the screeching of a rusty hinge. Startled and slightly dizzy, she looked around in wonderment, unable to believe her own eyes and ears and nose.

In all her nine years, she had never seen such a wretched place. An instant before, she had been snuggled under the wolfskin coverlet in her bed. Now she stood with pigs surrounding her, jostling her and crowding toward a trough. The sharp odor of pig manure choked her and turned her stomach. Pigs, here in her bedroom, in one of the finest houses in London? Pigs clambering over one another, threatening to knock her down and trample her? But this was surely not her bedroom.

"Sukie-e-e-e," she cried, but the snuffling and grunting and squealing of the pigs swallowed her voice. She clutched the handle of her music box and tucked Mariah tighter under her arm. Lifting her long velvet skirt with her free hand, she turned to

Response Notes

23

did she just wake up in her dream

from *Princess in the Pigpen*
by Jane Resh Thomas

gaze around her. Sukie had just now tucked her up in bed, and she couldn't remember going anywhere. What was she doing in a pigsty?

As she turned about, she saw a man standing in a shaft of sunlight that fell across the dusty room and struck Elizabeth's face. The man looked as shocked and bewildered as she felt. He was clearly a peasant, but not one of her father's servants—she knew them all.

Wiping away the tears on her cheeks with her sleeve, she mustered a commanding voice. "Who are you?" she demanded to know. "Take me back to my nurse this instant, or my father will have you hanged!"

At the same time, the man spoke, like the second lower voice in a duet. "Who are you, little girl, a princess? And what in blue blazes are you doing in there with my hogs?"

Elizabeth's head was swimming. Somehow she had flown from her own featherbed to this byre, where she struggled to keep her footing in a sea of pigs, Mariah under one arm, the walnut music box still pouring out its sweet song in her hand. It was as if no time had passed.

And this bold peasant was questioning her, a nobleman's daughter, in his strange kind of English. Father would certainly have this man killed. Or at least run out of London.

"You're in some pickle," said the man. As he closed a gate behind him and made his way across the pen, the pigs parted before him like the Red Sea. Elizabeth saw that he was wearing rough blue pantaloons and a waistcoat over a tartan blouse. Scots wore tartan—perhaps he was Scottish. He seemed poorly dressed in a foreign style, but his hair was golden and his smile kind.

A runty pig squealed and stood on its hind legs, imploring Elizabeth like a puppy to pick her up. She looked down at her favorite dress. The gold tracery Sukie had embroidered on the bodice and

she sounds spoiled - used to barking orders.

Is she dreaming?

24

from *Princess in the Pigpen*
by Jane Resh Thomas

sleeves glittered in the splinter of sun. But wherever the pigs had brushed against her, they had smeared and stained the claret velvet. 'Tis too late now to worry about soiling my gown, she thought.

"Sukie!" she called again. "Puck!" She had rarely in her life been out of Sukie's sight. As her fear mounted with the approach of the man, she cried out louder, demanding obedience. "Puck! Sukie!" Still no dog, no nurse. Here she stood, alone in a byre with a hundred pigs and a shabby peasant, not knowing how she had come there or where she was.

"Hold it, there. I don't bite, or even growl." The peasant picked her up and carried her out of the pigsty, while the music box played on, a feeble tinkle beneath the oinks and snorts of the pigs.

"Where did you come from, you and these fancy clothes?" The man set her gently on her feet and looked her up and down. "And where are your folks?"

"My father. . . ." said Elizabeth, struggling to calm her queasy stomach and rubbery legs. She took a deep breath and started again. "My father is Michael, Duke of Umberland, advisor to the Queen. Take me home at once!" Waving the music box like a scepter, she almost dropped Mariah in the steaming bucket of feed that stood by the gate.

giving orders

The man laughed. "And I," he said, one foot on the fence rail and his right hand on his chest, "I'm the King of England."

he's joking with her

Elizabeth gasped at the peasant's boldness. "Your head will look down from a pike on London Bridge this day," she said. "What is this place?"

"This? Why this is McCormicks' pig barn, in the state of Iowa. Joe McCormick, king of the pigs, at your service." As he made a little bow, a woman stepped through the open door, with the sun dazzling behind her, making a halo of her hair. "And this here's my queen, Queen Kathy."

his wife

25

●✎ Use clues in the story to make inferences.
Who is Elizabeth and how did she end up in Joe
McCormick's pig barn?

List three or four clues from the story that helped you
make your inferences about Elizabeth.

1.

2.

3.

4.

When you
read a story,
use the
information the author
provides to make
inferences about
characters and
their situations.

What's the Point?

When you read factual information, look for the main idea. The **main idea** is the central point that the author makes. Sometimes an author directly states the main idea. Other times you have to infer what the main idea is.

Begin by looking at the title and skimming the selection to discover the subject. Once you know what the subject is, you can find the main idea. Just ask yourself: What is the most important point that the author makes about this subject?

Read the following passage. When you know what the subject is, write it in the Response Notes. Then underline any important points the author makes about the subject.

from *Mistakes that Worked*
by Charlotte Jones

World War I lasted more than four years—from 1914 to 1918. During that time, approximately 8.5 million people were killed and 21 million were wounded.

Near the end of World War I, a doctor was walking outside a German military hospital with a soldier who had been blinded in battle. The doctor's dog joined the walk and when the doctor was called into one of the buildings, the blind soldier was left alone with the dog.

Soon the doctor returned, but the blind man and the dog were missing. When he found them, he discovered the dog had led the blind patient across the hospital grounds.

The doctor was amazed at what his untrained pet dog had done and decided to see how well a trained working breed of dog could lead a blind person. The results were great and the German government soon expanded the dog guide program.

An American woman named Dorothy Eustis visited Potsdam, Germany, to learn about the dog guide program. Through an article she wrote for *The Saturday Evening Post*, she brought the

Response Notes

from **Mistakes that Worked**
by Charlotte Jones

program to public attention in the United States. The first American dog guide school, The Seeing Eye, Inc., was established in 1929. Today ten major organizations train dogs and instruct blind people in their use.

The most popular breeds are German shepherds, golden retrievers, and Labrador retrievers. They must learn hand gestures and simple commands in order to lead the blind person across streets and around people, obstacles, holes, and low-hanging awnings or tree limbs.

The dog must also learn to exercise good judgment. If the blind person gives a "forward" command but the dog sees danger, the dog must know when to disobey. This is called "intelligent disobedience."

Dogs guiding blind masters is not new. Wall paintings, ancient scrolls, and legends tell of dogs leading blind men since 100 B.C. But until the German soldier was led by the doctor's untrained dog and the first training program was initiated, the incidents were scattered and the dogs were not always efficient.

In the case of dog guides, the old saying is true: A dog really is a man's—or a woman's—best friend.

Use the web below to jot down a few of the points the author makes about guide dog programs.

guide dog programs

Decide what the author's most important point is. Write the author's main idea below. Then write at least three supporting details the author has included.

Main Idea:

Supporting Details:

1.

2.

3.

4.

To identify the main idea of a piece of writing, ask yourself: What is the most important point the author makes about this subject?

29

4 What Does It Mean to Me?

Your response to what you read is as individual as your fingerprint. That's because each reader brings his or her own experiences, ideas, and feelings to the job of reading.

When you **reflect** on what you read, you think about what it means and explore your responses. What did I learn from this? How does this remind me of something I have experienced? How does this relate to my life?

As you read the next passage, pause once or twice to check your understanding of the author's meaning. In the Response Notes, jot down what you think the author means.

Response Notes

Always make time to really listen

About Loving by Jean Little

In my family, we don't talk much about loving.

My mother never bakes us pies or knits us socks. More than once, she's put cream in my father's coffee, although he takes it black. When she gets home from work she collapses, with her feet up. I have to shake her awake when it's time to eat.

My father never sends her roses or Valentines. He just says to her, "April, listen to this. April!" Then she yawns and opens half an eye and listens, while he reads her something by E. B. White or Tolstoy.

I listen, too. And they listen when I find something so perfect it must be shared. Nobody ever says, "Not now. I'm busy."

But nobody asks me about my homework either. And I do not wait to be told it's time for bed. If I want to floss my teeth, that's my affair. They couldn't care less.

I used to think they didn't know I was there. If I disappeared, I thought, they'd never notice.

But I was wrong.

About Loving by Jean Little

My father looks up, all at once, and asks me, "Katharine, tell me, what is truth?" And he doesn't go back to his book till he's heard my answer.

My mother does leave me to get the supper ready. But she brings me home ten brand-new drawing pencils.

Someday I'll send my mother one dozen roses. Someday I'll knit my father a pair of socks. When I have children I'll tell them, "It's time for bed."

But I'll also ask them sometimes, "What is truth?" And I'll leave them to get the supper and bring them pencils.

Loving isn't as simple as I once thought. Talking about it isn't what matters most.

What do you think the author's main point is?

Response Notes

teaching values

Doing, showing & being there for eachother is what matters most.

31

Reflect on your responses to this passage. How does it remind you of your own experience of family? Write a journal entry telling how the passage relates to your life.

32

After reading, take time to reflect on what you have learned and how it relates to your experiences.

Reading Fiction

[handwritten annotations:]
- fiction
- realistic fiction ⎫ could have
- historical fiction ⎭ happened - based on truth

Stories can introduce you to more places, times, people, adventures, and ideas than you could ever experience in your lifetime. The world of **fiction** includes places just like your neighborhood as well as the most fantastic lands you can imagine. It's inhabited by people just like you—and also by monsters, queens, wizards, giants, and talking animals.

All stories have certain elements in common. In this unit, you'll look at four of these elements: setting, character, plot, and theme. You'll see how writers use these elements to create imaginary stories that draw you in and seem as real as your own life.

[handwritten:] main idea, lesson, moral main point, meaning

In a Certain Place and Time

In every story, the action occurs in a certain place and time, which is called the **setting.** Authors frequently describe settings in great detail to make them seem real to readers. When you read a description of a setting, try to visualize it, or picture it in your mind. As you begin to form mental pictures of it, the setting will come alive.

In the story *The Wizard of Oz*, a tornado whirls a young Kansas girl and her dog into a magical place called the Land of Oz. As you read the passage, try to visualize the Emerald City. In the Response Notes, draw simple sketches of the place as you imagine it might appear.

Response Notes

from ***The Wizard of Oz*** by Frank Baum

THE WONDERFUL EMERALD CITY OF OZ

Even with eyes protected by the green spectacles Dorothy and her friends were at first dazzled by the brilliancy of the wonderful City. The streets were lined with beautiful houses all built of green marble and studded everywhere with sparkling emeralds. They walked over a pavement of the same green marble, and where the blocks were joined together were rows of emeralds, set closely, and glittering in the brightness of the sun. The window panes were of green glass; even the sky above the City had a green tint, and the rays of the sun were green.

There were many people—men, women, and children—walking about, and these were all dressed in green clothes and had greenish skins. They looked at Dorothy and her strangely assorted company with wondering eyes, and the children all ran away and hid behind their mothers when they saw the Lion; but no one spoke to them. Many shops stood in the street, and Dorothy saw that everything in them was green. Green sweets and green popcorn were offered for sale, as well as

from *The Wizard of Oz* by Frank Baum

green shoes, green hats, and green clothes of all
sorts. At one place a man was selling green
lemonade, and when the children bought it Dorothy
could see that they paid for it with green pennies.

There seemed to be no horses nor animals of
any kind; the men carried things around in little
green carts, which they pushed before them.
Everyone seemed happy and contented and
prosperous.

Response Notes

*Sounds very
different from
the movie setting.
—color green
—no animals*

Imagine that you are designing a book jacket cover
for *The Wizard of Oz*. Create a cover that shows the
Emerald City as you picture it from the author's
description.

35

Think about a fantasy place you would want to visit. Brainstorm what the sights, sounds, and smells of this place might be like. Then, in the space below, describe the setting for your fantasy story.

When you read a description of a setting, try to visualize the place in your mind.

Who's Who?

Characters are the people, animals, or imaginary creatures in a story. Some stories have characters who look, act, think, and feel just like you and other people you know. Other stories have characters who are more wild, funny, or heroic than anybody you know. Often authors try to create characters with whom readers can identify.

As you read the following passage, <u>look for clues to the personality of the main character</u>. Use a marker to highlight parts of the story that show <u>how the character acts, speaks, feels, or thinks</u>. In the Response Notes, jot down words that describe the character.

from *There's a Boy in the Girls' Bathroom*
by Louis Sachar

Jeff Fishkin was <u>hopelessly lost</u>. *feeling* He clutched his hall pass as he looked down the long empty corridor. The <u>school seemed so big to him</u>.

He was on his way to see the new counselor. She was supposed to help him "adjust to his new environment." Now he not only didn't know how to get to her office, he had no idea how to get back to Mrs. Ebbel's class either.

The floor was slippery. It had started raining during recess and the kids had tracked water and mud inside with them.

A teacher carrying a stack of papers stepped out of a door and Jeff hurried up to her. "Can you tell me where the counselor's office is, please?" he asked. <u>His voice trembled.</u> *action*

The teacher first checked to make sure he had a hall pass. Then she said: "The counselor's office . . . let's see. Go down this hall to the end, turn right, and it's the third door on your left."

"Thank you very much," said Jeff. He started to go.

Response Notes

Jeff—main character

actions—voice trembled
— slipped
— ran into girls room
— asked teacher for help

said— Oh no, thank you to teacher, huh?,
— asks where counselor is

Response Notes

feels - hopelessly lost

thinking - worst day
- lost, better,
embarrassed

embarrassed

38

from *There's a Boy in the Girls' Bathroom*
by Louis Sachar

"No, wait," said the teacher. "That's not right, she's in the new office in the other wing. Turn around and go back the way you just came, then turn left at the end of the hall and it's the second door on your right."

speaks "Thank you," Jeff said again.

He walked to the end of the hall, turned right, counted to the second door on his left, and pushed it open.

A girl with red hair and a freckled face was washing her hands at the sink. When she saw Jeff, her mouth dropped open. "What are you doing in here?" she asked.

"Huh?" Jeff uttered.

"Get out of here!" she yelled. "This is the girls' bathroom!"

Jeff froze. He covered his face with his hands, then dashed out the door.

"THERE'S A BOY IN THE GIRLS' BATHROOM!" the girl screamed after him.

He raced down the hall. Suddenly his feet slipped out from under him. He waved his arms wildly as he tried to keep his balance, then flopped down on the floor.

"Oh no, no, no, oh no, no, no," he groaned. "What have I done? Oh, why didn't I just read the sign on the door? This is the worst day of my whole life!"

What did you learn about Jeff? Complete the chart below by describing Jeff's personality traits. Then tell what actions, words, thoughts, or feelings demonstrate each trait.

brave, friendly
nice, honest, thoughtful, helpful, polite,
caring, responsible, respectful, confident,

Jeff's personality traits	Jeff's actions, words, thoughts, or feelings
Example: Fearful	His voice trembles.
embarrassed easily	felt horrible about wrong bath-room
responsible -	asks for directions
shy -	needs counselor to hp adjust
polite -	- please when asking directions, says thank you to teacher
confident -	once he got information
caring -	"what have I done?
trusting -	didn't look to read sign - just followed directions
nervous	voice trembling
happy	when he got directions

Try creating a character of your own. Below, make a list of your character's personality traits.

Character's Name

1.

2.

3.

39

Now describe how your character would act, think, and feel if he or she was lost on the first day of school. Write a paragraph telling how your character would have acted if he or she were in Jeff's situation.

As you read, think about what characters' actions, words, thoughts, and feelings reveal about them.

What Happens?

Besides characters and setting, stories also need a plot, or action. In most stories, the plot revolves around a problem and how it is solved. Readers often get wrapped up in the action of a story and begin to predict how the story will end.

As you read "The Birds' Peace," look for the problem. Once the problem becomes clear to you, jot it down in the Response Notes. Then write a prediction about how things will turn out.

"The Birds' Peace" by Jean Craighead George

On the day Kristy's father went off to war, she burst out the back door and ran down the path to the woods. Her eyes hurt. Her chest burned. She crossed the bridge over the purling stream and dashed into the lean-to she and her father had built near the edge of the flower-filled woodland meadow.

She dropped to her knees, then to her belly. Covering her face with both hands, she sobbed from the deepest well of her being.

Tears did not help. The pain went on and on.

A bird sang.

Kristy lifted her head. She recognized Fluter, the busy little song sparrow who lived in the bushes at the edge of the meadow. He seemed to be in trouble. His melodious song was loud and belligerent.

"I'm in trouble, too," she said. "My father had to go into the army. He's going to war. And I am scared." Fluter ignored her and sang on. From across the meadow, a strange song sparrow sang clearly and loudly. Kristy barely heard him.

"Daddy doesn't even know how to shoot a gun."

Fluter flew to a sumac bush, thrust out his spotted tan breast, and sang again.

"Suppose bombs fall on him." Kristy began to cry again. "Or an enemy tank shoots at him."

Response Notes

Kristy's dad is going to war + she's worried he's not prepared.

41

Response Notes

Birds - Fluter's area being intruded upon. (protect territory)

"The Birds' Peace" by Jean Craighead George

Fluter went on singing. After a few moments he flew across the meadow and boldly sang from a raspberry patch.

Dulce, his mate, flew off their nest in the thicket, where she had been incubating their eggs. She ate a bristlegrass seed and serenely preened her feathers. She was quite at ease.

Fluter was not. He turned this way and that. He flicked his tail and raised his crest, then flew to the bracken fern and sang. He flitted briskly to the sugar maple limb and sang from a conspicuous twig. He winged to the dogwood tree and sang from a high limb. As he flew and sang, Kristy became aware of what he was doing. He was making a circle, an invisible fence of song around his meadow and his nest in the thicket.

Suddenly Fluter clicked out what Kristy's father had told her were notes of warning. Dulce became alarmed. She flattened her feathers to her body and flew silently back to their nest.

Kristy checked to see what was the matter. The strange song sparrow was in Fluter's raspberry bush. He was pointing his bill at Fluter, who crouched as if he were going to fly at the stranger. But he did not. Instead, he sang.

The stranger heard Fluter's "stay-off-my-property" song and swiftly departed. He flew over Fluter's invisible fence of song and alighted on his own sapling. There he sang at Fluter.

Fluter flew to the sugar maple limb on the border of his territory and sang right back at him. The stranger answered with a flood of melody from his trees and bushes. When each understood where the other's territory lay, they rested and preened their feathers.

Kristy was fascinated. She sat up and crossed her legs.

"Even Daddy doesn't know about this," she said.

Putting her chin in her hands, she watched the birds until the day's long shadows told her she

"The Birds' Peace" by Jean Craighead George

must go home. And all that time, Fluter did not fly or sing beyond the raspberry bush, nor did the stranger come back to Fluter's territory. But sing they did, brightly and melodically, while their mates sat serenely on their brown-splotched eggs.

Dear Daddy, Kristy wrote that night. *I know how the birds keep the peace.*

predict - birds will
help Kristy
explain to her dad
how to solve a
problem without war.
(bird were at war)
(bird had to leave
family too)
- all they did
was talk.

 Summarize the story's plot by identifying the problem and its solution in the chart below.

Problem

Solution

43

➤ Extend the plot of this story. Imagine the note Kristy's dad might send back to her when he gets her note about the birds. Write his return note to her here.

Dear Kristy,

A story's plot usually involves a problem and its solution.

What's the Message?

Through the elements of setting, character, and plot, authors convey a **theme**—a statement about life or human nature. The theme is often a lesson that the reader learns from the story.

Usually a reader has to infer the theme from what happens in the story, though sometimes the author or a character directly states the theme. Because no two people read a story exactly the same way, different readers may find different themes in the same story.

Reread "The Birds' Peace" by Jean Craighead George. What important lesson does Kristy learn from the birds? This is the story's theme. Write the theme of "The Birds' Peace."

Connect this theme to your own life. Describe a situation or experience you've had that relates to the theme of "The Birds' Peace." What lesson about life did you learn from your experience?

46

To discover the
theme, ask yourself:
What lesson can I learn
from this story?

FOCUS ON EXPRESSION

Understanding Language

What makes a writer's work worth reading? A skilled writer not only has good ideas but also has an effective way of expressing them.

An active reader asks *what* an author has to say and studies *how* the author says it. In this unit, you'll focus on *how* authors express their ideas. You'll practice clarifying, visualizing, asking questions, and highlighting as you look at these different elements of language:

- tone
- metaphor
- personification
- sensory language

Expressing an Attitude

Read the two sentences below:

The school <u>forces</u> students to wear <u>plain</u> blue uniforms.

The school <u>provides</u> students with <u>stylish</u> blue uniforms.

Notice how the choice of words conveys a negative attitude in the first sentence and a positive attitude in the second. The attitude an author conveys in a piece of writing is called **tone**.

Think about the author's tone as you read this passage about a Chinese girl who comes to live in Brooklyn, New York, in 1947. The teacher in the story is telling her students about Jackie Robinson, the first African American to play baseball in the major leagues. In the Response Notes, write down adjectives that describe the tone of the story.

Response Notes

smile

①

from *In the Year of the Boar and Jackie Robinson*
by Bette Bao Lord

"Baseball is not just another sport. America is not just another country. . . ."

If Shirley did not understand every word, she took its meaning to heart. Unlike Grandfather's stories which quieted the warring spirits within her with the softness of moonlight or the lyric timbre of a lone flute, Mrs. Rappaport's speech thrilled her like sunlight and trumpets.

"In our national pastime, each player is a member of a team, but when he comes to bat, he stands alone. One man. Many opportunities. For no matter how far behind, how late in the game, he, by himself, can make a difference. He can change what has been. He can make it a new ball game.

"In the life of our nation, each man is a citizen of the United States, but he has the right to pursue his own happiness. For no matter what his race,

from *In the Year of the Boar and Jackie Robinson*
by Bette Bao Lord

religion or creed, be he pauper or president, he has the right to speak his mind, to live as he wishes within the law, to elect our officials and stand for office, to excel. To make a difference. To change what has been. To make a better America.

"And so can you! And so must you!"

Shirley felt as if the walls of the classroom had vanished. In their stead was a frontier of doors to which she held the keys.

"This year, Jackie Robinson is at bat. He stands for himself, for Americans of every hue, for an America that honors fair play.

"Jackie Robinson is the grandson of a slave, the son of a sharecropper, raised in poverty by a lone mother who took in ironing and washing. But a woman determined to achieve a better life for her son. And she did. For despite hostility and injustice, Jackie Robinson went to college, excelled in all sports, served his country in war. And now, Jackie Robinson is at bat in the big leagues. Jackie Robinson is making a difference. Jackie Robinson has changed what has been. And Jackie Robinson is making a better America.

"And so can you! And so must you!"

Suddenly Shirley understood why her father had brought her ten thousand miles to live among strangers. Here, she did not have to wait for gray hairs to be considered wise. Here, she could speak up, question even the conduct of the President. Here, Shirley Temple Wong was somebody. She felt as if she had the power of ten tigers, as if she had grown as tall as the Statue of Liberty.

metaphor

metaphor

49

👉 **What four or five words would you use to describe the tone of the passage?**

Strong

excel

proud

confident

better life

👉 **First decide who or what the subject of this passage is. Then state the author's attitude toward the subject. Finally, select three examples from the passage that reveal the author's attitude.**

Subject: Jackie Robinson - how one person can make a difference.

Author's Attitude: Can make a difference no matter your background.

Example: citizen of U.S. w/ rights: to pursue own happiness
right to speak your mind - creed, religion, pauper

Example: Despite of humility + injustice went to college

Example: Shirly is an immigrant - she is somebody who can also make a difference

➤ Write two paragraphs about baseball or another sport. In the first paragraph, convey a positive tone and in the second a negative one.

Positive tone *Michelle Kwan – winning her 5th World title in March of 2003.*

51

Negative tone *Skating and judging – very political*

Through word choice, an author conveys a tone, or attitude, toward a subject.

Vivid Comparisons

Basketball is a break dance; baseball is a waltz.

What strikes you about this sentence? It compares two sports to dances, creating metaphors. A metaphor is a direct comparison of two things. <u>It says one thing *is* another.</u> Writers use metaphors to create vivid pictures in a reader's mind or to capture the essence of something. For example, basketball is a fast-paced game with quick moves and jumps, like a break dance. But baseball is slow-paced, like a waltz.

When you read a metaphor, try to picture it in your mind. Think about the similarities between the two things being compared. Now read the poem below and underline the metaphors. Use the Response Notes to sketch what you visualize.

Response Notes

The Sidewalk Racer *or* On the Skateboard
by Lillian Morrison

<u>Skimming</u>
<u>an asphalt sea</u> (sidewalk)
I swerve, I curve, I
sway; I speed to whirring
sound an inch above the
ground; <u>I'm the sailor</u>
<u>and the sail,</u> <u>I'm the</u>
<u>driver and the wheel</u>
<u>I'm the one and only</u>
<u>single engine</u>
<u>human auto</u>
<u>mobile.</u>

➤ Think about the metaphors in the poem. How are the two things the author compares alike? Reflect on the metaphors and explain their meanings in the chart below. The first one is done for you.

Things Compared	Likenesses
sidewalk is compared to an **asphalt sea**	"Skimming an asphalt sea" Both stretch on and on. You can glide over both.
How is the **skateboarder** is compared to the **sailor and the sail** ?	"I'm the sailor and the sail" The skateboard gliding over the pavement is like a boat gliding on water.
skateboarder is compared to the **driver and the wheel**	"I'm the driver and the wheel" The skateboarder is like a car driver because he also too controls his turns and speed.
skateboarder is compared to a **human automobile**	"I'm the one and only human automobile."

53

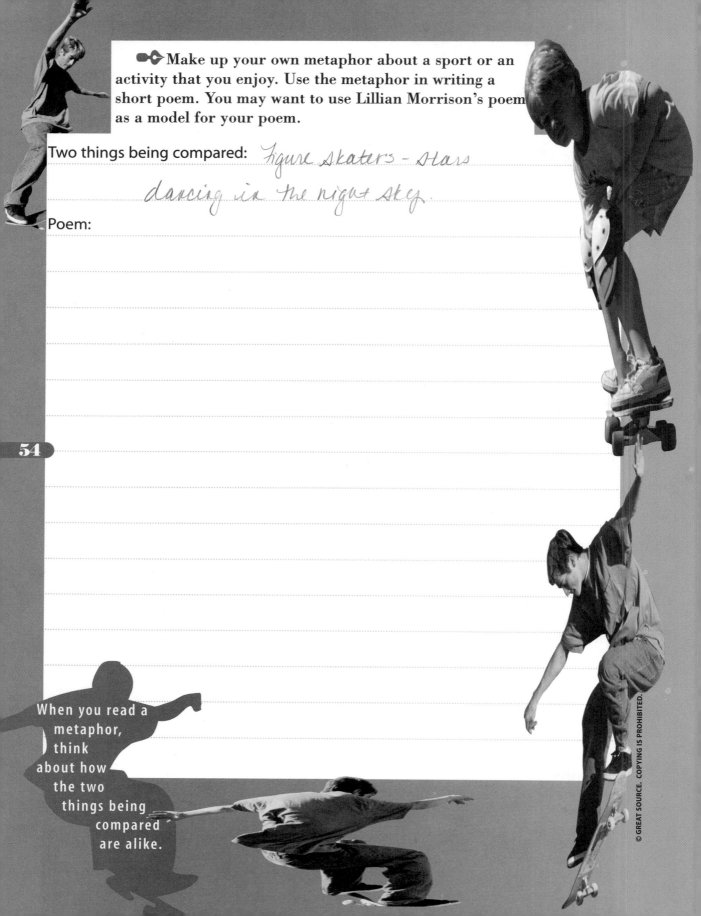

Make up your own metaphor about a sport or an activity that you enjoy. Use the metaphor in writing a short poem. You may want to use Lillian Morrison's poem as a model for your poem.

Two things being compared: *Figure skaters - stars dancing in the night sky.*

Poem:

When you read a metaphor, think about how the two things being compared are alike.

Appearing Human

If people can act like animals, can animals act like people? Writers think so. When a writer gives a human trait—the ability to speak, think, feel, or act like a person—to an animal or any non-human thing, it's called **personification.**

As you read "Desert Tortoise," ask yourself: What human traits does this animal have? Jot down your answers in the Response Notes.

Desert Tortoise by Byrd Baylor

Response Notes

I am the *old* one here.

speaks in first person

Mice
and snakes
and deer
and butterflies
and badgers
come and go.
Centipedes
and eagles
come and go.

but I live longer

But tortoises
grow old
and *stay.*

Our lives stretch out.

I cross
the same arroyo
that I crossed
when I was young,
returning to
the same safe den
to sleep through
winter's cold.

Desert Tortoise by Byrd Baylor

Each spring,
I warm myself
in the same sun,
search for the same
long tender blades
of green,
and taste the same
ripe juicy cactus fruit.

I know
the slow
sure way
my world repeats itself.
I know
how I fit in.

My shell still shows
the toothmarks
where a wildcat
thought he had me
long ago.
He didn't know
that I was safe
beneath
the hard brown rock
he tried to bite.

scars from life

I trust that shell.
I move
at my own speed.

This
is a good place
for an old tortoise
to walk.

◗━◗In what ways is the tortoise like a very old person?

Tortoise

live long -others come+go
creeps along slowly

Old person

long life
walks slowly

◗━◗Think about a pet or a favorite animal. On the lines below, list ways in which the animal acts or seems human.

57

Human quality:

likes to take naps

Human quality:

likes good food

Human quality:

likes to cuddle and be loved

Animal:

cat

Human quality:

likes to be independent

Human quality:

gets scared at loud noises

➥ Now try using personification in your own writing. Use the animal you wrote about on the previous page. Write a speech in which the animal tells you what it appreciates about its life.

see p. 113 teacher guide

58

When you read an example of personification, ask yourself: What human traits does this non-human thing have?

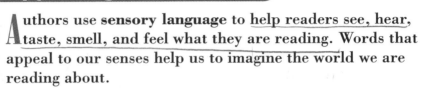

4 ⟩ Appealing to the Senses

Authors use **sensory language** to <u>help readers see, hear, taste, smell, and feel what they are reading.</u> Words that appeal to our senses help us to imagine the world we are reading about.

Read this passage about a newborn bat named Shade once just to see what happens. Then read it again, this time highlighting examples of sensory language. In the Response Notes, write *see*, *hear*, *taste*, *smell*, or *feel* next to each example you underline.

from ***Silverwing*** by Kenneth Oppel

Response Notes

see
<u>Skimming</u> over the banks of the stream, Shade *sound* <u>heard</u> the beetle warming up its wings. He flapped harder, picking up speed as he homed in on the *sound* <u>musical whine.</u> He was <u>almost invisible against the night sky, the streaks of silver in his thick black fur flashing in the moon's glow.</u> *see*

    sight
    sight
    touch

Airborne now, the beetle was a whirl of shell and wing. Shade still couldn't see it with his eyes— but he could see it with his ears. Caught in his echo vision, the insect hummed and <u>glowed in his mind</u> *smile* <u>like a shadow edged in quicksilver.</u> <u>The air whistled in his flared ears</u> as he swooped down. Braking sharply, he scooped the beetle up with his tail membrane, flicked it into his left wing, and volleyed it straight into his open mouth. He veered up and away, and <u>cracked the hard shell</u> with his teeth, *taste* savoring the delicious beetle meat as it <u>squirted down his throat.</u> After a few good chomps, he swallowed it whole. Very tasty. <u>Beetles were far and away the best food in the forest.</u> Mealworms and midges weren't bad either. Mosquitoes didn't really taste like much—gauzy, <u>a little prickly at times</u>—but they were also the easiest to catch. He'd already eaten over six hundred this evening, something like that anyway, he'd lost count. They were so slow and clumsy all you had to do was keep your mouth open and swallow every once in a while.

    sound

    sound
    touch

    taste

    touch

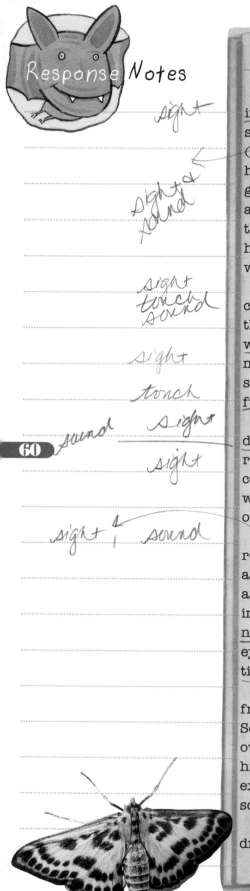

Response Notes

sight

sight & sound

sight touched sound

sight

touch

sound *sight*

sight

sight & sound

from **Silverwing** by Kenneth Oppel
personification

He spun out a web of sound, searching for insects. He was starting to feel full, but he knew he should be eating more. His mother had told him (she'd been telling him for the past ten nights) he had to get fat, because winter was coming. Shade grimaced as he snatched a mealworm from a leaf and gulped. As if he could ever be fat! He knew, though, that there was a long journey ahead of him, south to Hibernaculum where the whole colony would spend the winter.

All around him in the crisp autumn night, he could hear and see other Silverwings streaking through the forest, hunting. Shade stretched his wings luxuriously, only wishing they were longer, more powerful. For a moment he closed his eyes, sailing by sound alone, feeling the air caress the fur of his face and stomach.

His ears pricked suddenly. It was the telltale drumming of a tiger moth in flight. He tilted his right wing and wheeled, locking onto his prey. If he could just catch one—everyone knew how hard they were to catch—and then he'd have a story of his own to tell back at Tree Haven at sunrise.

There it was, chopping its gossamer wings, rocking clumsily. It was laughable, really. He was almost upon it, and maybe this wasn't so hard after all. He cast a net of sound around it and drew in his wings for the plunge. But a hailstorm of noise tore apart his echo vision, and in his mind's eye, he suddenly saw not one but a dozen silvery tiger moths, all veering in different directions.

Shade blinked in confusion. The moth was still in front of him—he could see it with his eyes. Somehow it was scrambling up his echoes with its own. Use your eyes, just your eyes now, he told himself. He flapped harder, coming in fast, claws extended. Wings billowing, he pulled back, and scooped his tail forward to catch his prize when—

The tiger moth simply folded shut its wings and dropped straight down out of his path.

from **Silverwing** by Kenneth Oppel

Shade was going too fast, and he couldn't stop. His tail just swept right round underneath him, and he flipped. Clawing air, he plummeted for a split second before righting himself. He cast around for the tiger moth in amazement.

Above him it fluttered along placidly.

"Oh, no you don't!"

He beat his wings and climbed swiftly, gaining. But another bat suddenly flashed in front of him, snapping the tiger moth into his mouth.

"Hey!" cried Shade. "That was mine!"

"You had your chance," said the other bat, and Shade recognized his voice instantly. Chinook. One of the other newborns in the colony.

"I had it," Shade insisted.

"Doubt it." Chinook chewed vigorously and let the wings flutter from his teeth. "This is fabulous, by the way." He made exaggerated smacking sounds. "Well, maybe you'll get lucky one of these nights, Runt."

Response Notes

sight

sound — sight

sight,

see, taste

sound

61

🖐 After reading this passage, what do you think a bat's life is like?

see p. 115 teacher guide

🖐 With a friend, list three examples of sensory language from the story. Then tell whether each example appeals to the sense of sight, sound, taste, smell, or touch.

Examples of sensory language   Sense or senses

1.

2.

3.

➤ Continue the story of Shade by describing another experience the bat has. Use language that helps your reader see, hear, smell, feel, or taste what is happening.

Sensory language helps a reader see, hear, feel, taste, and smell what the author is describing.

Reading Authors: Phyllis Reynolds Naylor

Author Phyllis Reynolds Naylor spends about six hours writing each day. She works on ideas in her mind while she swims, hikes, and cooks. "It's as though pressure builds up inside me and writing even a little helps to release it."

Like all writers, Naylor has her bad days. Yet she never gives up, even if it takes more than a year to write one book.

Moreover, she believes in herself. She has received more than *10,000 rejections* from publishers in her life. But she has also published more than 100 books and won countless awards. What's her advice? Pick a topic you like—even if no one else likes it— then "take a cup of hot chocolate, settle down in a comfortable chair," and write, write, write.

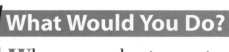

What Would You Do?

When you read a story, put yourself in the character's shoes. First, think about the character's situation or problem. Then think about similar experiences in your own life. Use the information in the story and your own experience to predict what characters will do and how the story might turn out.

You've probably never eaten a beetle. Still, you can make some predictions about what might happen in this excerpt from *Beetles, Lightly Toasted*. What would you do if you were given an assignment like that of Andy? What do you think will happen after he mails the letter? Write your ideas in the Response Notes.

Response Notes

from *Beetles, Lightly Toasted*
by Phyllis Reynolds Naylor

The way Andy figured it was this: if the population ever grew so big that there wasn't enough food to feed everybody, then people could save their lives by eating things they hadn't thought of eating before. Things like lizards and snakes and grasshoppers. Not that *Andy* would eat them, of course, but some day, if people were starving, *somebody* might.

Start with what you have and see how far you can stretch it, Mr. Sudermann had said. *Put your imaginations to work.* Maybe you didn't have to be starving. Maybe, if you were just poor or you wanted to save money on your grocery bill, you could find stuff to eat in your own backyard.

Andy knew that primitive tribes ate things like grubs, which was just like eating worms. He had heard about fancy stores selling chocolate-covered ants as a novelty item. But no one he knew, except the yellow cat, had ever made a meal out of beetles. The first thing he had to do was find out exactly what could be eaten safely. Wendell had told him once that a university was a place where you could find out anything you wanted to know, so Andy wrote a letter to Iowa State University:

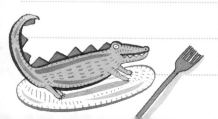

from **Beetles, Lightly Toasted** by Phyllis Reynolds Naylor

Dear Sir:

I am writing an essay for a contest and I need to know what bugs and things you can eat. And worms too. How do you know if they are poison or not? How do you fix them? Please answer soon.

Yours truly,
Andy Moller

On the envelope he wrote, "Department of Bugs," and then he added the address he had copied from the catalog in Wendell's room, with his own address in the corner.

Aunt Wanda saw him putting on the stamp. "Who's the letter to?" she asked, as she carried her jade plant to a sunny place on the window ledge.

"Oh, somebody," Andy told her.

"Well, most letters *are* to somebody," she said, and cast him a strange look.

Andy walked down to the end of the lane toward the mailbox.

●◆ **What do you think will happen after Andy sends the letter? Write your prediction below.**

If someone from the "Department of Bugs" writes back, what will he or she say? Draft a short note here.

Dear Andy,

66

When you read, try to think ahead in the story and predict what will happen.

Recipe for Writing

Phyllis Naylor came up with the idea for *Beetles, Lightly Toasted* one day while reading the local paper. In the paper, she came across a recipe for chili—using chopped up earthworms. Ms. Naylor wasn't thrilled with the thought of eating earthworm chili, but she *loved* the recipe as an idea for writing.

Writers often get ideas for writing from things they read or hear about. Read the next passage from *Beetles, Lightly Toasted* to see how Phyllis Naylor used her imagination to build on the newspaper story she read. What did Phyllis Naylor add to the newspaper story about earthworm chili? What did she change? Jot down your reactions to the story in the Response Notes.

from ***Beetles, Lightly Toasted*** (continued)
by Phyllis Reynolds Naylor

Response Notes

On May 1, when Andy had about given up ever hearing from the University, there was a letter for him in the box, and he was glad he had found it before anyone else did:

Dear Andy:

Your letter asking about bugs and things has been given to me for reply, and I hope I will be able to help. Probably most insects are edible, especially their larvae or pupae. But because some of them—especially brightly-colored insects—might have poisons in their bodies, it would be best to stick with crickets, grasshoppers, and ordinary brown beetles.

Ant and bee larvae are also a good source of fat and protein; meal worms, often found where grain is stored, are delicious, I understand, fried in garlic butter. To prepare insects for eating, put them on a diet of cornmeal for a few days to rid their digestive tracts of grit, then cook.

from **Beetles, Lightly Toasted** by Phyllis Reynolds Naylor

Earthworms can also be put on a diet of applesauce, then simmered until tender. Grasshoppers, crickets, and beetles, lightly toasted, with the legs and wings removed, add crunch to a recipe, and can be used in place of nuts for brownies.

If you don't like the idea of dropping live worms and insects in boiling water, you might put them in a covered box in the freezer first, then cook them later. Good luck on your essay, and *bon appetit!*

Cordially,
John Burrows, Entomologist

Andy understood the whole letter except the last two words before "cordially."

"Mom," he said that evening as he worked his arithmetic problems on the kitchen table, and she sat across from him going over her poultry and egg records, "What does *bon appetit* mean?"

"Bon appetit?" Mother looked up. "It's French, Andy. It means 'good appetite' or 'good eating.' 'Enjoy your meal'—something like that."

Andy kept one hand tightly over his mouth and said nothing.

In what ways did Professor Burrows's answer to Andy surprise you?

68

Often, writers keep track of ideas for stories by writing them down. Look through your local newspaper for interesting headlines. Note possible story ideas. Below, write some of the best ideas you find.

Suppose Andy decides to try one of Professor Burrows's cooking ideas. Put together a recipe you think Andy might use. Feel free to borrow ideas from Professor Burrows's letter.

69

Recipe for

Writers sometimes find funny or interesting ideas for stories in unexpected places.

3 Conflict: It's Essential

What do you think of when you hear the word *conflict?* Maybe you think of an argument, or even a physical fight. Some conflicts *are* physical, but many happen as a "war of ideas" inside a character's mind. Sometimes characters struggle simply to make the right decision. Conflict is essential to almost every good story.

As you read the passage from *Boys Against Girls*, look for moments of conflict. Highlight these moments. Then, in the Response Notes, jot down your thoughts about how each conflict might be resolved.

Response Notes

from ***Boys Against Girls*** by Phyllis Reynolds Naylor

Wally Hatford usually spent the day after Halloween counting his trick-or-treat candy, trading off Mars bars for Milky Ways, and opening all the little packets of candy corn. He'd pop a whole handful into his mouth at once, and follow that with a couple of chocolate kisses.

But not this Halloween.

Wally and his two older brothers, Jake and Josh, sat numbly in the living room, looking at the candy wrappers scattered about the floor after their party for the girls—the party the Malloy girls had tricked them into giving. Never mind that the Hatford brothers had tried to trap them in the cemetery and would have dropped worms on their heads if they'd succeeded. The fact that the girls had found them out and beaten them at their own game was too humiliating for words.

"You know what I wish?" said Jake after a while. "I just wish a big tornado would sweep through Buckman and blow them away. Not kill them exactly—just deposit them back in Ohio where they belong."

"I wish there would be a big flood and they'd just wash away," said Josh, his eleven-year-old twin.

from **Boys Against Girls** by Phyllis Reynolds Naylor

Seven-year-old Peter was eating a malted milk ball he'd found under the couch. He'd had no part in the trickery, so his conscience was clear. "What do you wish, Wally?" he asked.

Wally wished, quite frankly, that his brothers would quit asking him questions, that's what. He always got dragged into things whether he wanted to be or not. And right now he did not want to be.

He was tired of girls. Sick of girls. Bored to death with talking about them. Since the Hatfords' best friends had moved to Georgia and rented out their house to the Malloys, it had been "the Malloy girls this" and "the Malloy girls that," and if Jake and Josh hated them so much, why were they always talking about them, looking at them, laughing at them, and thinking about what they were going to do next? It was disgusting.

"Well?" said Jake and Josh together, still waiting for his answer.

Wally had to say something. He sighed. "I wish the abaguchie would carry them off," he said finally.

What moments of conflict did you notice in this story? Write down two or three. How was each conflict resolved?

1.	Conflict	Resolution

2.	Conflict	Resolution

3.	Conflict	Resolution

Describe a conflict you've had with a family member, a friend, or within yourself. Explain how the conflict was resolved.

73

Look for physical or mental conflicts in stories and note how they are resolved.

4 An Author's Style

An author's style is created by the choices he or she makes in writing. These choices include the kinds of words the writer uses, the type of dialogue, the amount of description, and the tone of the writing.

If you have strong feelings when you read the following passage from *Shiloh*, no wonder. It's based on a real experience when Phyllis Naylor found a sad, frightened dog. "That dog so haunted me," she said, "that long after we came home, I knew I had to write about her."

Read the story and circle words and phrases that create strong feelings in you. In the Response Notes, jot down the emotions you felt.

Response Notes

74

from **Shiloh** by Phyllis Reynolds Naylor

When I turn around and the dog sees me coming, he goes off into the woods. I figure that's the last I'll see of the beagle, and I get halfway down the road again before I look back. There he is. I stop. He stops. I go. He goes.

And then, hardly thinking on it, I whistle.

It's like pressing a magic button. The beagle comes barreling toward me, legs going lickety-split, long ears flopping, tail sticking up like a flagpole. This time, when I put out my hand, he licks all my fingers and jumps up against my leg, making little yelps in his throat. He can't get enough of me, like I'd been saying no all along and now I'd said yes, he could come. It's a he-dog, like I'd thought.

"Hey, boy! You're really somethin' now, ain't you?" I'm laughing as the beagle makes circles around me. I squat down and the dog licks my face, my neck. Where'd he learn to come if you whistled, to hang back if you didn't?

I'm so busy watching the dog I don't even notice it's started to rain. Don't bother me. Don't bother the dog, neither. I'm looking for the place I first

Response Notes

from *Shiloh* by Phyllis Reynolds Naylor

saw him. Does he live here? I wonder. Or the house on up the road? Each place we pass I figure he'll stop—somebody come out and whistle, maybe. But nobody comes out and the dog don't stop. Keeps coming even after we get to the old Shiloh schoolhouse. Even starts across the bridge, tail going like a propeller. He licks my hand every so often to make sure I'm still there—mouth open like he's smiling. He is smiling.

Once he follows me across the bridge, though, and on past the gristmill, I start to worry. Looks like he's fixing to follow me all the way to our house. I'm in trouble enough coming home with my clothes wet. My ma's mama died of pneumonia, and we don't ever get the chance to forget it. And now I got a dog with me, and we were never allowed to have pets.

If you can't afford to feed 'em and take 'em to the vet when they're sick, you've no right taking 'em in, Ma says, which is true enough.

I don't say a word to the beagle the rest of the way home, hoping he'll turn at some point and go back. The dog keeps coming.

I get to the front stoop and say, "Go home, boy." And then I feel my heart squeeze up the way he stops smiling, sticks his tail between his legs again, and slinks off. He goes as far as the sycamore tree, lies down in the wet grass, head on his paws.

"Whose dog is that?" Ma asks when I come in.

I shrug. "Just followed me, is all."

"Where'd it pick up with you?" Dad asks.

"Up in Shiloh, across the bridge," I say.

"On the road by the river? Bet that's Judd Travers's beagle," says Dad. "He got himself another hunting dog a few weeks back."

"Judd got him a hunting dog, how come he don't treat him right?" I ask.

"How you know he don't?"

"Way the dog acts. Scared to pee, almost," I say. Ma gives me a look.

75

from **Shiloh** by Phyllis Reynolds Naylor

"Don't seem to me he's got any marks on him," Dad says, studying him from our window.

Don't have to mark a dog to hurt him, I'm thinking.

"Just don't pay him any attention and he'll go away," Dad says.

"And get out of those wet clothes," Ma tells me. "You want to follow your grandma Slater to the grave?"

I change clothes, then sit down and turn on the TV, which only has two channels. On Sunday afternoons, it's preaching and baseball. I watch baseball for an hour. Then I get up and sneak to the window. Ma knows what I'm about.

"That Shiloh dog still out there?" she asks.

I nod. He's looking at me. He sees me there at the window and his tail starts to thump. I name him Shiloh.

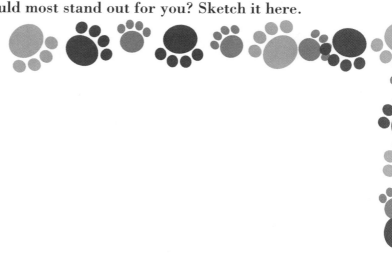

If you were to close your eyes and think about this story without looking back at the words, what one image would most stand out for you? Sketch it here.

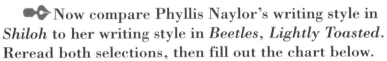 Reflect on the writing style Naylor uses in this passage from *Shiloh*. Read the following statements about Naylor's style and circle your answer choices.

Naylor uses words that are:	simple	fancy	somewhere in between
The dialogue in *Shiloh* sounds like:	everyday speech	formal speech	somewhere in between
In this passage, the amount of description is:	heavy	light	somewhere in between
The tone of this story makes me feel:	happy	sad	somewhere in between

 Now compare Phyllis Naylor's writing style in *Shiloh* to her writing style in *Beetles, Lightly Toasted*. Reread both selections, then fill out the chart below.

	word choice	dialogue	description	tone
Beetles, Lightly Toasted				
Shiloh				

✒ Write a paragraph comparing Phyllis Naylor's writing style in *Beetles, Lightly Toasted* with her writing style in *Shiloh*. Use your chart on page 77 to examine Naylor's word choice, dialogue, description, and tone in the two selections.

An author's style can affect how readers feel about characters and events in stories.

Reading Well

Have you ever considered how much you'd miss out on if you couldn't read? In this unit, you'll learn about how orphans were treated a hundred years ago, where you can see huge piles of snakes, the true risk a tarantula poses, and how one young girl feels about racism.

As you read about these topics, you'll also learn about ways to become a more effective reader. You will identify main ideas and details, summarize, ask questions, and make inferences. These strategies will help increase your understanding and enjoyment of what you read.

Getting the Whole Picture

hen you read factual writing, one of your tasks as a reader is to identify the main idea and the details. The **main idea** is the most important idea, or central point. The **details** are facts or sentences that support or tell more about the main idea. Picture the main idea as the hub of a wheel and the details as the spokes.

Sometimes writers directly state the main idea in one or more sentences, as the author does in the following passage from *Orphan Train Rider*. After you read the passage once, go back and circle the main idea and underline the key details.

Response Notes

from *Orphan Train Rider* by Andrea Warren

More than 200,000 children rode "orphan trains" in this country between 1854 and 1930. They were part of a "placing out" program created to find homes for children who were orphans or whose parents could not take care of them.

Most of the riders came from New York or other large cities in the East. The trains brought groups of them to other parts of the country where they were lined up in front of crowds of curious onlookers. Interested families could then choose the child they wanted. Within a week a child could go from living in an orphanage or on city streets to living in a Midwestern farmhouse or village. Many children found parents who loved them and took care of them; others never felt at home with their new families. Some were mistreated.

There is not much time left for orphan train riders to tell their stories. Those still alive are now elderly. Some will not talk about their experiences because they feel ashamed of being a "train kid" or because they did not find a happy home at the end of their ride. Others, like Lee Nailling . . . believe that it is important for Americans to know about the orphan trains and the children who rode them.

Do the orphan trains sound like a good idea? Why or why not?

In your own words, state the main idea of this passage on the center of the wheel. Note five details—sentences that tell more about the main idea—on the outer part of the wheel.

Detail

Detail

Detail

Main Idea

Detail

Detail

When you read nonfiction, find the main idea and the details that support or tell more about the main idea.

2 Summing It Up

A good way to remember what you have read is to summarize it. When you **summarize,** you state the main idea and most important details in your own words. A summary is usually short, perhaps a paragraph or two long. It doesn't include everything—just the most important information.

The following passage is from a book about Bob Mason, a scientist who studies snakes and works to protect them. As you read the passage, pause from time to time to check your understanding of the main idea. In the Response Notes, jot down the most important information in your own words.

Response Notes

from *The Snake Scientist* by Sy Montgomery

Every spring for the past fifteen years, Bob has flown halfway across the continent to the windswept Canadian prairie to study the red-sided garters. Every time he comes, he's dazzled again by the spectacle.

"This is the most awesome, remarkable sight I've seen in my life!" Bob says. Though garter snakes are among the most common snakes in the world, nowhere else do they gather in numbers like this.

No wonder the snakes of Narcisse have become a tourist attraction. Schoolbuses unload some four hundred kids a day in the spring as teachers bring their classes to see them. Parents come pushing babies in strollers.

"These snakes are tremendous ambassadors to the rest of the world for snakes," Bob says, as he allows a snake to slither from one hand into the other. "They're harmless, cute, and fascinating."

If you come to Narcisse, park guides will tell you the rules of snake den etiquette.

Be careful where you step. There might be a snake underfoot.

Don't disturb a big group of snakes or pick up a mating pair.

from *The Snake Scientist* by Sy Montgomery

Never run or chase others with snakes.

If you pick up a snake, hold it gently with two hands. Allow it to move freely by letting it slide out of one hand and into the other, like a Slinky.

Always put snakes back where you found them.

A second grader with red hair and freckles holds a wild snake in her hands for the first time. "I used to hate snakes, but now I love them!" she says, delighted with her discovery. "They're soft and not slimy!"

Rick Shine, a snake specialist from Australia, is also delighted to see so many snakes. He's traveled here to help Bob study these animals. "I can see more snakes in a day here than in the course of a three-year field study," he says.

Why are there so many snakes in one place? Snakes, like all reptiles, are cold-blooded creatures whose body temperature rises and falls with the weather. They warm up with the sun and cool down when temperatures drop. In the winter they can't put on warm parkas, so they need to find a place to stay where they won't freeze.

Usually snakes crawl into small holes or basements or barns for the winter. Some dig little burrows beneath the frost line. But here, sixty miles north of Winnipeg, the special geology of the area lets some red-sided garters spend the winter at the world's biggest slumber party.

Two feet beneath the topsoil, this land is made of limestone, a soft rock that is dissolved slowly by streams and rivers to form great underground caves. In places these caves have collapsed, producing rubble-filled sinks shallow enough for snakes to crawl in and out. Some sinks are small, sheltering a few hundred snakes. But the three large dens at Narcisse are big enough for tens of thousands at a time. They pack in so thickly that they're stacked in piles on top of one another.

**Use your notes to summarize this article. Write the most important point (the main idea) in the box. Then list three details that support the main idea.

Main Idea:

1.

2.

3.

Imagine that you are visiting Narcisse over spring break. Use your summary and notes to write a postcard to a friend, describing what you have seen.

85

Summarizing helps you understand and remember what you read.

3 Asking Questions

When you take a trip, you probably have lots of questions about the place you're going. What does it look like? What can I do there? What's the weather like? How long will it take to get there? Your questions help you anticipate what the trip will be like.

Asking questions before you read helps you anticipate what you'll discover, too. It sets a direction and gives a purpose for your reading.

The following passage is about tarantulas, or giant spiders. Before you begin reading, write down any questions you have about tarantulas in the left column of the chart below. Then read the passage to see if any of your questions are answered. Underline the answers you discover.

TARANTULAS

Questions I have	What I found out

from *The Tarantula* by Gail LaBonte

Long ago in Taranto, a small town in Italy, the people enjoyed dancing to lively music at their village's many festivals. Perhaps because they spent so much time celebrating and not enough time working, the government passed a law against dancing.

The people of Taranto did not want to give up their fun. Instead, they invented a story about a big spider that was often seen near their town. They said the only way to survive this spider's bite was to dance wildly enough to sweat out its deadly poison.

Soon, the villagers were dancing again. Over time, this dance came to be called the *tarantella*, and the spider became known as the tarantula.

The villagers had a good time fooling the government with their trick. However, the poor spider never lost its reputation for being scary.

When explorers from Europe reached the New World, they were frightened by the even larger spiders they found there. They called these spiders "tarantulas," too, and the name stuck.

Surprisingly, the spider of Taranto, Italy, is not closely related to the spiders that modern-day scientists call tarantulas. The Italian creature is really a wolf spider. Like a real wolf, it travels away from its home, hunting for food. A wolf

87

from ***The Tarantula*** by Gail LaBonte

spider is big but looks tame compared to the hairy giants now known as tarantulas.

SCARY BUT SHY

The giant spiders of the New World looked very dangerous to the European explorers centuries ago. Like these explorers, many people today wonder how dangerous tarantulas really are.

People do not need to worry about tarantulas. They don't usually attack animals larger than themselves. The bite of a tarantula is poisonous enough to kill insects, lizards, frogs, baby birds, and small rodents, but not humans.

Go back to the chart on page 86 and write the answers you found in the passage.

What information in the article surprised you? Why?

➤ Think of a topic you are interested in learning more about. Write the topic and the questions you have about it in the chart. Then find information about your topic in an encyclopedia, at the library, or on the Internet. Add your answers to the chart.

Topic:

Questions I have	Answers I found

Asking questions before you read helps give you a purpose for reading.

Active readers take what the author says and make inferences about the author's meaning. **Inferences** are *reasonable* guesses. They are based in part on information the author provides and in part on what the reader already knows.

The following passage comes from a book in which kids talk about their true-life experiences with prejudice. As you read, jot down inferences in the Response Notes about what kind of person Yingyi is. Underline the information you based your inferences on.

CHINA

Response Notes

from *Under Our Skin: Kids Talk About Race*
by Debbie and Tom Birdseye

I was born in the Guangdong area of China, in the southern tip, pretty close to Hong Kong. I don't have any brothers or sisters. You're only supposed to have one child in China.

I've been in America about four years and am now in middle school. I like to play softball and volleyball and other sports. I play the piano, too, and I'm going to be taking clarinet. Bach's my favorite composer. I like to collect stamps and have a collection of Chinese stamps because we get mail from China sometimes.

When I get home from school I have to do homework. Afterwards, I like to curl up in my bedroom and read. I love mysteries. Sometimes I like ghost story mysteries.

I can't read in Chinese, though. I have this special book that my mom teaches me out of. I'm memorizing the characters. I know probably one hundred. You need to know about two thousand to be able to read the Chinese newspaper.

from ***Under Our Skin: Kids Talk About Race***
by Debbie and Tom Birdseye

My mom is learning English, so we speak both English and Chinese at home. Sometimes I say everything in Chinese except one word, because I can't think of it right then. I speak English more than I speak Chinese, because I'm at school more than I'm at home.

It's different being Chinese. I feel special. We use chopsticks when we eat. We don't use knives and forks. It gives me privileges, too. I can go to different special things that are Chinese, like the Chinese New Year, or special holidays. And sometimes I can dress in special clothes, and get to visit a place like Beijing. China is really, really big.

I think of myself as more American than Chinese, though. I used to use my Chinese name, Yingyi. But sometimes I was teased about it. I tried to just either ignore it, or I said to them, "I bet if you went to China people would tease you about your name, because your name would seem different." Maybe then they'd find out how bad teasing is. But then I thought, Jenny sort of sounds like Yingyi. If I was Jenny nobody would tease me. So now when people ask, I say my name is Jenny.

Some people just don't accept you for who you are. Since you don't look like them, they think you don't belong with them, like you're different inside, too. I look Chinese, and I might have an accent. Some people make fun of others because they have an accent. I think it's unfair. What would they

91

PAKISTAN

from *Under Our Skin: Kids Talk About Race*
by Debbie and Tom Birdseye

think if they were trying to speak, and they had a little accent? Would they want everybody to laugh at them like they laugh?

Everybody's personality is different. The way they think is different, and their culture is different. But just because they look different on the outside, they are still human beings. You just have to respect other people's rights. If you see someone who is really different, you should try to be friends. They might be really interesting. It might open you to another world.

I have a lot of American friends, but also friends who have different backgrounds. I have a best friend at school from England. Her name is Rose. I have friends from Nepal, Mexico, and Russia. I have a friend from Pakistan—Marium. She dresses in her culture's clothes almost every day. She tells me about her country and her different holidays and about the god she worships and stuff like that. I like meeting people from other countries, how each one is different from each other. It doesn't matter what their race or color is, I accept them for who they are.

⬤➤ Yingyi says, "If you see someone who is really different, you should try to be friends." Explain why you agree or disagree with this statement.

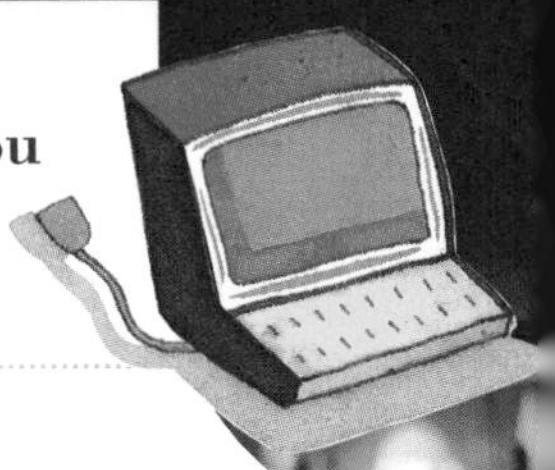

_____

_____

_____

_____

_____

⬤➤ Describe what Yingyi is like in the chart below.

What does she like to do?

What is her personality like?

What makes her special?

Yingyi

What are her beliefs?

Pretend you are Yingyi. Write a journal entry telling about a time at school someone made fun of you. Make inferences about how this would feel. Describe the feelings in the journal entry.

JOURNAL

Use the information an author provides to make inferences about people or situations.

Reading Nonfiction

Nonfiction writing is about things that really happened—or are about to happen. It can be every bit as <u>exciting</u> as any fictional story, and no wonder. It's about real life.

However, nonfiction writers cannot simply make something up when they run out of ideas. They need to dig for the facts so that what they write will be real. At the same time, they need to make the facts both convincing and interesting. As you read the nonfiction selections in this unit, ask yourself whether these writers have done a good job of <u>bringing the facts to life.</u>

to make it interesting and exciting to read

First, Next, and Last

Nonfiction can be organized in many ways. Some nonfiction writers write about events in the order that they happen. This is called **time-order sequence**.

In his biography of Abraham Lincoln, author Russell Freedman uses sequence to build suspense. The details and facts build slowly to the most important event—the peak. As you read the following passage, notice the order in which events occur. Number them in the Response Notes.

Response Notes

①After dinner-going to theatre. Lincoln, his wife, Mjr. Rathbone Miss Harris

96

② Arrival @ theatre

③ Watching play

④ Guard left, door unlocked-noticed

⑤ Shadowy figure
to build suspense
↳ burst into
balcony + shot pres.

⑥ Struggle- Rathbone / assailant

⑦ Assailant escapes

pictures tell the story

from **Lincoln: A Photobiography** by Russell Freedman

After dinner, Lincoln and Mary left for Ford's Theatre in the company of a young army major, Henry R. Rathbone, and his fiancee, Clara Harris. Arriving late, they were escorted up a winding stairway to the flag-draped presidential box overlooking the stage. The play had already started, but as Lincoln's party appeared in the box, the orchestra struck up "Hail to the Chief" and the audience rose for a standing ovation. Lincoln smiled and bowed. He took his place in a rocking chair provided for him by the management and put on a pair of gold-rimmed eyeglasses he had mended with a string. Mary sat beside him, with Major Rathbone and Miss Harris to their right.

The play was _Our American Cousin,_ a popular comedy starring Laura Keene, who had already given a thousand performances in the leading role. Lincoln settled back and relaxed. He laughed heartily, turning now and then to whisper to his wife. Halfway through the play, he felt a chill and got up to drape his black overcoat across his shoulders.

During the third act, Mary reached over to take Lincoln's hand. She pressed closer to him. Behind them, the door to the presidential box was closed but not locked. Lincoln's bodyguard that evening, John Parker, had slipped away from his post outside the door to go downstairs and watch the play.

coln: A Photobiography by Russell Freedman

...udience had just burst into laughter when
...swung open. A shadowy figure stepped
...box, stretched out his arm, aimed a small
... pistol at the back of Lincoln's head, and
... trigger. Lincoln's arm jerked up. He
...forward in his chair as Mary reached out
...him. Then she screamed.

Major Rathbone looked up to see a man standing
with a smoking pistol in one hand and a hunting
knife in the other. Rathbone lunged at the gunman,
who yelled something and slashed Rathbone's arm
to the bone. Then the assailant leaped from the box
to the stage, twelve feet below. One of his boot
spurs caught on the regimental flag draped over
the box. As he crashed onto the stage, he broke the
shinbone of his left leg.

The assailant struggled to his feet, faced the
audience, and shouted the motto of the
commonwealth of Virginia: _"Sic semper tyrannis"_—
(Thus always to tyrants). The stunned and
disbelieving audience recognized him as John
Wilkes Booth, the well-known actor. What was going
on? Was this part of the play?

Booth hobbled offstage and out the stage door,
where a horse was saddled and waiting. Twelve
days later he would be
cornered by federal
troops and shot in a
Virginia barn.

The theatre was in
an uproar. People were
shouting, standing on
chairs, shoving for the
exits, as Laura Keene
cried out from the
stage, "The president
is shot! The president
is shot!"

97

SIC SEMPER TYRANNIS

Complete the following chart. Track five of the key events leading up to the assassination of President Lincoln. The first event and the last (peak) event have been filled in for you.

Peak Event:

President Lincoln is shot.

Event 5

Event 4

Event 3

Event 2

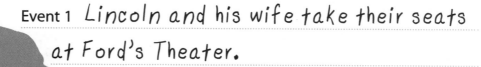

Event 1 Lincoln and his wife take their seats at Ford's Theater.

98

Authors use time-order sequence to help readers keep track of events and to build suspense.

In Your Own Words

One way to keep track of information is to summarize what you read. When you **summarize**, you write down the key events or most important ideas from your reading in a paragraph or two.

The story of Lincoln's assassination is continued below. As you read the rest of the excerpt, again pay attention to the sequence of events. Jot down notes about key events in the Response Notes. Decide which event is the *peak*—the most important event—and put a star by it.

from ***Lincoln: A Photobiography*** (continued)
by Russell Freedman

Response Notes

99

(1) Two doctors rushed to the president's box. Lincoln had lost consciousness instantly. The bullet had entered his skull above his left ear, cut through his brain, and lodged behind his right eye. The doctors worked over him as Mary hovered beside them, sobbing hysterically. Finally, six soldiers (2) carried the president out of the theatre and across the fog-shrouded street to a boardinghouse, where a man with a lighted candle stood beckoning. He was placed on a four-poster bed in a narrow room off the hallway. The bed wasn't long enough for Lincoln. He had to be laid diagonally across its cornhusk mattress.

(3) Five doctors worked over the president that night. Now and then he groaned, but it was obvious that he would not regain consciousness. The room filled with members of the cabinet, with congressmen and high government officials. Mary waited in the front parlor. "Bring Tad—he will speak to Tad—he loves him so," she cried. Tad had been attending another play that evening. Sobbing, "They killed my

from *Lincoln: A Photobiography* (continued)
by Russell Freedman

pa, they killed my pa," he was taken back to the White House to wait.

Robert Lincoln was summoned to join the hushed crowd around his father's bedside. Outside, cavalry patrols clattered down the street. Another assassin had just tried to murder Secretary of State William Seward. Everyone suspected that the attacks were part of a rebel conspiracy to murder several government officials and capture the city.

By dawn, a heavy rain was falling. Lincoln was still breathing faintly. Robert Lincoln surrendered to tears, then others in the room began to cry. At 7:22 A.M. on April 15, Lincoln died at the age of fifty-six. A doctor folded the president's hands across his chest. Gently he smoothed Lincoln's contracted face muscles, closed his eyelids, and drew a white sheet over his head. It was then that Secretary of War Edwin M. Stanton murmured, "Now he belongs to the ages."

➡️ Use the notes you made while reading to fill in this chart about the events leading up to the president's death. The first and last events have been filled in for you.

Peak Event:

President Lincoln dies.

Event 5

Event 4

Event 3 members of family come, Congress

Event 2 carry Lincoln across st. to be worked on

Event 1 After being shot, the president loses consciousness.

101

Pretend you have been asked to investigate the events leading up to President Lincoln's assassination. Review both excerpts again. Then write an official summary of your "findings." Remember, a summary includes only the most important facts and is written in your own words.

Official Report

on the Death of President Lincoln

Prepared by:

102

Summarizing can help you understand and keep track of what you read.

3 Examining Cause and Effect

Some nonfiction pieces are organized by time order, or sequence. Other nonfiction describes cause and effect relationships. This means that one event makes one or more other events occur.

The following excerpt from *A River Ran Wild* tells the history of the Nashua River and the land around it. In the Response Notes, write down what <u>important changes take place in the river and land</u>. These are the *effects*. To get at *causes*, ask yourself <u>why these changes occurred</u>. When you find causes in the text, circle them.

Response Notes

from ***A River Ran Wild*** by Lynne Cherry

One day a group of native people, searching for a place to settle, came upon the river valley. From atop the highest mountain, known today as Mt. Wachusett, they saw the river nestled in its valley, a silver sliver in the sun.

They came down from the mountain, and at the river's edge they knelt to quench their thirst with its clear water. Pebbles shone up from the bottom.

"Let us settle by this river," said the chief of the native people. He named the river Nash-a-way— River with the Pebbled Bottom.

By the Nash-a-way, Chief Weeawa's people built a village. They gathered cattails from the riverbanks to thatch their dwellings. In the forest they set fires to clear brush from the forest floor. In these clearings they planted corn and squash for eating. They made arrows for hunting and canoes for river travel.

When the Indians hunted in the forest or caught salmon in the river, they killed only what they needed for themselves for food and clothing. They asked all the forest creatures that they killed to please forgive them.

The Nashua people saw a rhythm in their lives and in the seasons. The river, land, and forest provided all they needed.

from **A River Ran Wild** by Lynne Cherry

The Nashua had lived for generations by the clear, clean, flowing river when one day a pale-skinned trader came with a boatload full of treasures. He brought shiny metal knives, colored beads, and cooking kettles, mirrors, tools, and bolts of bright cloth. His wares seemed like magic. The Nashua welcomed him, traded furs, and soon a trading post was built.

The settlers built fences for their pastures, plowed the fields, and planted crops. They called the land their own and told the Indians not to trespass. Hunting land disappeared as the settlers cleared the forest. Indian fishing rights vanished as the settlers claimed the river.

The Indians' ways were disrupted and they began to fight the settlers. The wars raged for many years but the Indians' bows and arrows were no match against gunpowder, and so the settlers' rifles drove the Indians from the land.

Through a hundred years of fighting, the Nashua was a healthy river, sometimes dammed for grist and sawmills, but still flowing wild and free. Muskrats, fish, and turtles still swam from bank to bank. Deer still came to drink from the river, and owls, raccoons, and beaver fed there.

At the start of the new century, an industrial revolution came to the Nashua's banks and waters. Many new machines were invented. Some spun thread from wool and cotton. Others wove the thread into cloth. Some machines turned wood to pulp, and others made the pulp into paper. Leftover pulp and dye and fiber was dumped into the Nashua River, whose swiftly flowing current washed away the waste.

These were times of much excitement, times of progress and invention. Factories along the Nashua River made new things of new materials. Telephones and radios and other things were made of plastics. Chemicals and plastic waste were also dumped into the river. Soon the Nashua's fish and wildlife grew sick from this pollution.

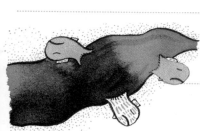

from ***A River Ran Wild*** by Lynne Cherry

One night Oweana, a descendant of Weeawa who still lived by the Nashua, had a dream so vivid that he awoke in wide-eyed wonder. In his dream Chief Weeawa's spirit returned to the river and saw it as it was now—still and deadly.

Chief Weeawa mourned for the Nash-a-way, but where his tears fell upon the dirty waters, the waters were cleansed until the river once again flowed freely.

The next morning Oweana went to speak to his friend Marion. When he told her of his dream, she said, "I had this dream also! River with the Pebbled Bottom is the name Weeawa gave it, but today no pebbles shine up through the Nashua River's waters." Together they decided something must be done.

Marion traveled to each town along the Nashua. She spoke of the river's history and of her vision to restore it. "No longer do we have a river—it's a stinking, smelly sewer. But it wasn't always this way."

People listened and imagined a sparkling river, full of fish. They imagined pebbles shining up through clear waters. They signed petitions and sent letters. They protested to politicians and showed them jars of dirty water. They convinced the paper mills to build a plant to process the waste. They persuaded the factories to stop dumping. Finally, new laws were passed and the factories stopped polluting.

Slowly, slowly, the Nashua's current began to clean its water. Year by year the river carried away the dyes and fiber to the ocean. Marion and Oweana thanked the people who had helped to clean the Nashua.

Through the meadows, towns, and cities, the Nashua once again flows freely. Paper pulp no longer clogs it. Chemicals no longer foul it.

Now we walk along its banks and row upon its fragrant waters. We can set our boats upon it and with its current, drift downstream.

105

> ■►Review the events that take place in *A River Ran
> Wild* by filling in the cause-and-effect map below.

(important changes)

Causes (why)	Effects
Chief Weeawa's people settle by the river.	
White traders come and settle by the river.	
Wars rage between the Indians and the white settlers.	
	The Nashua's fish and wildlife grow sick from pollution.
	New laws are passed and factories stop polluting.
	The Nashua flows freely and people are once again able to enjoy the river.

106

In the space below, create a drawing about what happened to the Nashua River. Include at least one cause and one effect in your drawing.

When you read nonfiction, look at what events happen, then ask yourself what caused them to happen.

4 Fiction Based on Fact

Fiction is writing about imaginary people and events. Nonfiction is writing about real people and real events. **Narrative nonfiction** combines elements of both kinds of writing. Fictional elements include dialogue and characters' inner thoughts. Nonfictional elements include historical facts, such as names, dates, and places.

The following excerpt is about a real person—an 18th century African prince who was captured by slave traders and brought to Massachusetts. As you read, mark three or four parts of the story that appear to be based on historical facts and three or four parts that appear to be fictional. Write *fact* or *fiction* in the Response Notes near these parts.

Response Notes

"At-mun" from *Amos Fortune, Free Man*
by Elizabeth Yates

The *White Falcon* sailed slowly up the coast. It put in at different ports and dropped off anywhere from fifty to sixty blacks at a time, depending on the need for labor and the price they could fetch. The graceful white-winged bird approached her home port of Boston on the first Sunday in July of the year 1725. The master gave orders to furl sail and ride at anchor outside the harbor until the next day. More than one slaver had been forced to go elsewhere because she had tried to land her cargo on a Sunday.

When the ship drew up to her wharf on Monday morning, twenty slaves—all that remained of her human cargo—were brought up on deck. Among them were the strongest, those least impaired by the voyage and those best able to stand the rugged New England climate. At-mun looked into their faces. Not one of them were of the At-mun-shi. Where his people were now, he did not know.

The gestures, not the words, of the mate made the Africans understand that they were to walk down the gangplank to the wharf. They moved slowly because of their chains, docilely because of the lash that could cut their naked skin as quickly

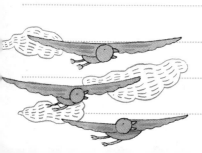

"At-mun" from *Amos Fortune, Free Man*
by Elizabeth Yates

as it could the air. A crowd of people had already gathered near the auction block, men for the most part. But a few curious women hovered on the outskirts. At-mun was hailed by the auctioneer and his chains were removed. For the first time in more than four months he could walk freely, yet not freely. He had been given a pair of trousers to wear before coming off the ship and he found them even more restrictive than chains. The people on the wharf shouted with laughter at the curious way the black youth walked. At-mun mounted the block. Above him, gulls were dipping and soaring, coming to rest in the tall masts of the *White Falcon*, filling the air with their raucous cries. At-mun kept his eyes on them.

"Here's a fine specimen of the Gold Coast," the auctioneer began, slapping At-mun's shoulder and running his hands down the strong arms, the trousered legs. "Well-limbed, not much more than a boy, capable of years of hard work, lusty, strong, sound in health. Remember what you get when you get them young. You can train them the way you want them to go."

A voice shouted out from the crowd.

The auctioneer cupped his ear to hear better. "Defects? Why, none at all. Can't you see for yourself?" Then he consulted a paper the mate had given him describing the *Falcon's* merchandise. "Wait a moment now. It says here that this one can't talk. Is that so?" He peered at At-mun towering above him and barked up into his face, "Come on, now. Let's hear you say something."

At-mun continued to watch the gulls.

The auctioneer shrugged his shoulders. "That ought to put his price up. Think of having a black who can't talk back to you once he learns English!"

The crowd roared with laughter.

A man dressed in gray and wearing a broad-

"At-mun" from *Amos Fortune, Free Man*
by Elizabeth Yates

brimmed hat stepped forward. He looked up at the auctioneer. "What is the youth's name?" he asked.

The auctioneer laughed. "Name? None of them have any names."

The man went to the foot of the block and looked up at At-mun. "What is your name?" he asked.

At-mun had never heard anything come from a white man's lips but commands, curses, threats, none of which he understood. He brought his gaze from the gulls to the face of the man addressing him, for the words just spoken were different in tone. At-mun had no comprehension of their meaning but he understood the look in the man's eyes. He had never answered a white man. He had vowed to himself that he never would. But his lips opened and the word that came through them was "At-mun."

The man in gray turned to the auctioneer. "Friend, will thee take £30 and do no bidding on this man?"

The auctioneer thought for a moment, realizing that he was being offered almost twice what he had hoped to get even with bidding for the truculent black.

"He's yours," he said.

The money was paid and the slave led down from the block.

"He looks an intelligent lad," the purchaser commented.

The auctioneer did not answer until he had pocketed his money. "That will wear away soon enough," he said. "Give him plenty of hard work and you'll soon have him in the shape you want him."

"At-mun," the slave said again, wanting to add that he was a king but the words had gone from him. His own name and the dwindling dust of a few memories was all that he had brought with him from his home land.

➥ Examine the historical parts of the narrative by filling in the chart below.

Who:

What Happened:

When:

Where:

➥ Now summarize the story—or narrative:

In the beginning . . .

Then . . .

Finally . . .

●━○ Now try making some inferences about At-mun. Use information from the text and your own experiences to answer the following questions:

1. What do you think At-mun thought and felt as he mounted the auction block?

....

....

....

....

....

....

2. What do you think At-mun felt after he was sold?

....

....

....

....

....

....

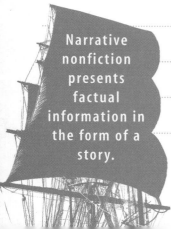

Narrative nonfiction presents factual information in the form of a story.

Understanding Language

A writer's language and craft are as individual as his or her personality or facial expressions. The language a writer chooses can create a mood, cause an emotional response, or create a picture in the reader's mind.

In this unit, you'll have a chance to explore how different writers use language. As you read the selections in this unit, take a close look at these elements of each author's language:

- word choice
- imagery
- style
- description

Playing with Words

Writers know that language is a powerful tool. Words can be used in many ways—for example, to teach, to persuade readers, or to evoke specific emotions. Sometimes writers use words in unexpected ways in order to entertain readers.

As you read *My Life as a Fifth-Grade Comedian,* notice how Bobby uses words in surprising ways to make his classmates laugh. Mark any parts of the story that make *you* laugh. In the Response Notes, jot down why you found certain parts funny.

Response Notes

from *My Life as a Fifth-Grade Comedian*
by Elizabeth Levy

Mr. Matous can be pretty funny. He *likes* to laugh. Some teachers don't, but when you get one who does, you're golden. It's Mr. Matous's first year of teaching. He's the kind of teacher who thinks all kids are worth saving. Everybody in the class knows that I am the type of kid who is too much for Mr. Matous to handle. It's made for an interesting year.

"Hand your homework assignments up to the front," said Mr. Matous. My classmates were smirking. I could tell they were just waiting for what I would do next. I wouldn't disappoint them. I always come up with something. One by one, my classmates gave their homework to Mr. Matous—everyone except me. "Bobby," said Mr. Matous. He sounded tired. "Did you do your homework?"

"No," I admitted. "I did some other kid's homework."

The class tittered. "Bobby, that joke is so old, it has mold on it," said Mr. Matous.

The class laughed hysterically. That's what I love about Mr. Matous. He's as funny as I am. "Quiet!" he shouted. "It wasn't that funny. Bobby, this is the third time in a row that you haven't done your homework. What's the problem?"

"It's not a good time in my life for homework right now." The class cracked up again.

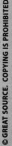

from *My Life as a Fifth-Grade Comedian*
by Elizabeth Levy

"Now what exactly does that mean?" asked Mr. Matous.

"I mean, there's a lot going on at home right now. I don't have time for homework."

Mr. Matous looked confused. I tend to have that effect on teachers. "Class, open your history books and review the chapter on Columbus's first encounters with Native Americans," he said. He came down the aisle and stood in front of my desk with a concerned look on his face. "What's happening at home that's keeping you from doing your homework?" he asked softly. "If there's really a problem, you know that you can come to me."

I thought about it. First-year teachers are such suckers for hard-luck stories. I could tell him about Jimmy's fight with my parents after he got kicked out of school. I looked out the window. It was a cold March day. I was supposed to meet Jimmy after school. Jimmy's almost eighteen—eight years older than me. He's staying with a friend. I miss him. Home is not exactly a barrel of laughs without Jimmy. He left home, and my parents won't ask him back. They call it tough love, but it seems like tough luck to me. I can just imagine what will happen to me when I step out of line. The wind was blowing. A gust of wind hit a piece of newspaper and sent it tumbling up into the air—as if the laws of gravity had been turned upside down.

"What problems?" repeated Mr. Matous.

"Uh, seriously, Mr. Matous," I said in a loud voice so the other kids could hear, "I would have done my homework, but there was a problem in my house. They cut off the gravity. Dad forgot to pay the bill. He's very absentminded."

I could hear some of my classmates giggling. It was a sound I loved.

"Cut off the gravity," repeated Mr. Matous. Most adults would ask, "Is that supposed to be a joke?"

115

HISTORY COLUMBUS

from **My Life as a Fifth-Grade Comedian**
by Elizabeth Levy

Not Mr. Matous. He was having a hard time keeping a straight face.

"Yeah, things are pretty up in the air right now." I love it when jokes come to me. I'd have to add this one to my notebook. I write down the best jokes that I've heard or made up. I've got a whole shelf full of books on how to be a comic, and they all say the same thing—keep a notebook with you at all times to jot down ideas. But this idea was more than just a joke. I wished something like that could really happen—gravity cutting off. All my problems would float up and away.

What is Bobby like? What do you think of him?

What he says:	How others feel about him:

Bobby

How he feels:	What I think about him:

➦ Read the sentences on the left from the story. On the right, explain how the words make you feel.

Sentences from story	What I feel ...
"Bobby, that joke is so old, it has mold on it," said Mr. Matous.	
He left home, and my parents won't ask him back. They call it tough love, but it seems like tough luck to me.	
I wished something like that could really happen—gravity cutting off. All my problems would float up and away.	

117

Writers use words in unexpected ways to surprise readers and create humor.

Bringing Writing to Life

"The five-foot rattler inched over the sand silently, its gaze never moving from the desert rat."

Does this sentence create a picture in your mind? Details like "inched over the sand" help us see what is happening, and even make us worry a little over what's going to happen next. Lively details and sharp pictures keep you alert, as a good reader should be.

Read this passage from "Spaghetti." When a sharp image catches your attention, underline it. Note how it makes you feel in the Response Notes.

Response Notes

from "Spaghetti" by Cynthia Rylant

It was evening, and people sat outside, talking quietly among themselves. On the stoop of a tall building of crumbling bricks and rotting wood sat a boy. His name was Gabriel and he wished for some company.

Gabriel was thinking about things. He remembered being the only boy in class with the right answer that day, and he remembered the butter sandwich he had had for lunch. Gabriel was thinking that he would like to live outside all the time. He imagined himself carrying a pack of food and a few tools and a heavy cloth to erect a hasty tent. Gabriel saw himself sleeping among coyotes. But next he saw himself sleeping beneath the glittering lights of a movie theater, near the bus stop.

Gabriel was a boy who thought about things so seriously, so fully, that on this evening he nearly missed hearing a cry from the street. The cry was so weak and faraway in his mind that, for him, it could have been the slow lifting of a stubborn window. It could have been the creak of an old man's legs. It could have been the wind.

But it was not the wind, and it came to Gabriel slowly that he did, indeed, hear something, and that it did, indeed, sound like a cry from the street.

When images are strong, chances are the words that created them are strong, too. Look at the words or passages you marked. List two of your favorites here.

1.

2.

Draw a picture to go with one of the images created by Cynthia Rylant's words. Sketch it here the way you see it in your mind.

Writers use strong words to paint strong images.

3 The Writer's Style

J ust as you have your own fingerprints, you have your own writing style. Every writer does. The words you choose and the way you use them in your writing help define your style. It might be flowing and flowery. It could be crisp and concise. Some writers are very direct. Others make us think and work hard to figure out the meaning of their words. As you read the rest of "Spaghetti," think about the author's style. Underline or highlight any words or expressions you feel are part of her "writer's fingerprints."

Response Notes

from **"Spaghetti"** (continued) by Cynthia Rylant

Gabriel picked himself up from the stoop and began to walk carefully along the edge of the street, peering into the gloom and the dusk. The cry came again and Gabriel's ears tingled and he walked faster.

He stared into the street, up and down it, knowing something was there. The street was so gray that he could not see. . . . But not only the street was gray.

There, sitting on skinny stick-legs, wobbling to and fro, was a tiny gray kitten. No cars had passed to frighten it, and so it just sat in the street and cried its windy, creaky cry and waited.

Gabriel was amazed. He had never imagined he would be lucky enough one day to find a kitten. He walked into the street and lifted the kitten into his hands.

Gabriel sat on the sidewalk with the kitten next to his cheek and thought. The kitten smelled of pasta noodles, and he wondered if it belonged to a friendly Italian man somewhere in the city. Gabriel called the kitten Spaghetti.

Gabriel and Spaghetti returned to the stoop. It occurred to Gabriel to walk the neighborhood and look for the Italian man, but the purring was so loud, so near his ear, that he could not think as seriously, as fully, as before.

from **"Spaghetti"** (continued) by Cynthia Rylant

Gabriel no longer wanted to live outside. He knew he had a room and a bed of his own in the tall building. So he stood up, with Spaghetti under his chin, and went inside to show his kitten where they would live together.

Response Notes

➡➤ Reread the passage. Take another look at Cynthia Rylant's style. Fill out the following chart by circling any choices with which you agree. Then add some ideas of your own.

The tone of this story is _____.

funny   serious   silly

scary   gloomy   thoughtful

Other words that describe Rylant's tone:

The sentences in this story are mostly _____.

long   short   complicated   simple

Other words that describe Rylant's sentences:

The descriptions in this story are _____.

flowery   direct   detailed

clear   colorful   plain

Other words that describe Rylant's descriptions:

➥ Write a review of "Spaghetti" that focuses on the author's style:

1. Choose one paragraph from the story.

2. Describe the author's tone, word choices, and descriptions.

3. Then tell why you did or did not like the author's style.

122

An author's style is his or her own unique way of using language.

Descriptive Language

Good writing helps us see things in our minds as clearly as we see them in real life. In addition, sharp images create feelings—for many reasons. Perhaps the writer uses words that create a particular mood. Or perhaps a description calls up a memory that brings strong feelings with it.

As you read the following passage from *Tuck Everlasting*, mark any descriptive words and images you find. In the Response Notes, jot down your thoughts or feelings about the images.

from *Tuck Everlasting* by Natalie Babbitt

The first week of August hangs at the very top of summer, the top of the live-long year, like the highest seat of a Ferris wheel when it pauses in its turning. The weeks that come before are only a climb from balmy spring, and those that follow a drop to the chill of autumn, but the first week of August is motionless, and hot. It is curiously silent, too, with blank white dawns and glaring noons, and sunsets smeared with too much color. Often at night there is lightning, but it quivers all alone. There is no thunder, no relieving rain. These are strange and breathless days, the dog days, when people are led to do things they are sure to be sorry for after.

One day at that time, not so very long ago, three things happened and at first there appeared to be no connection between them.

At dawn, Mae Tuck set out on her horse for the wood at the edge of the village of Treegap. She was going there, as she did once every ten years, to meet her two sons, Miles and Jesse.

At noontime, Winnie Foster, whose family owned the Treegap wood, lost her patience at last and decided to think about running away.

Response Notes

123

from **Tuck Everlasting** by Natalie Babbitt

And at sunset a stranger appeared at the Fosters' gate. He was looking for someone, but he didn't say who.

No connection, you would agree. But things can come together in strange ways. The wood was at the center, the hub of the wheel. All wheels must have a hub. A Ferris wheel has one, as the sun is the hub of the wheeling calendar. Fixed points they are, and best left undisturbed, for without them, nothing holds together. But sometimes people find this out too late.

What two descriptive images from the story stand out most for you? How did they make you feel?

Image #1   Feelings

Image #2   Feelings

Choose any month OTHER than August. Brainstorm some descriptive words and images that come into your mind as you think of this month. Write the month you chose on the hub of the wheel below. Then write the words and images you think of on the spokes coming out from that hub.

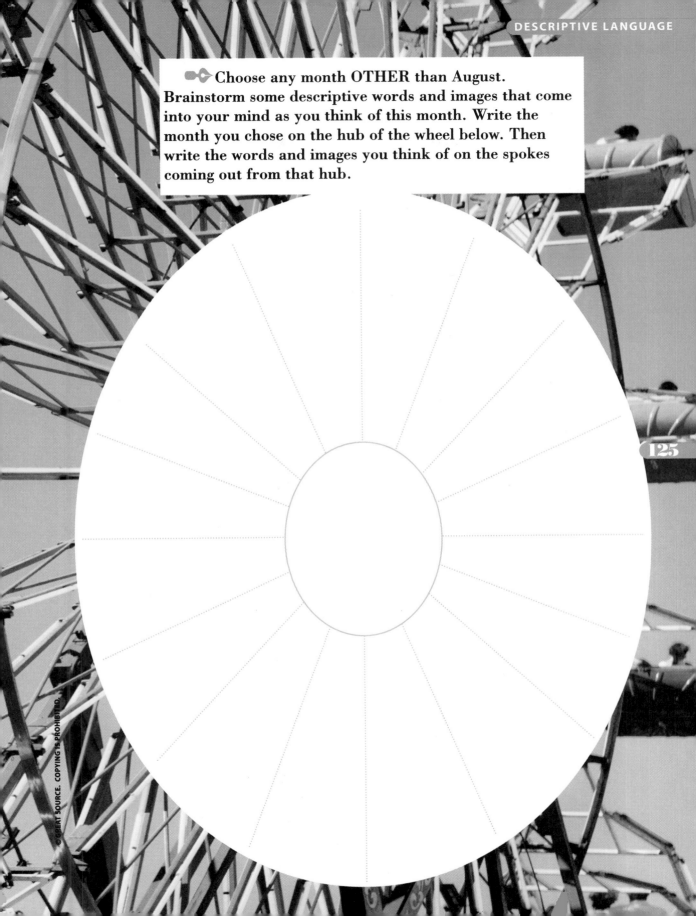

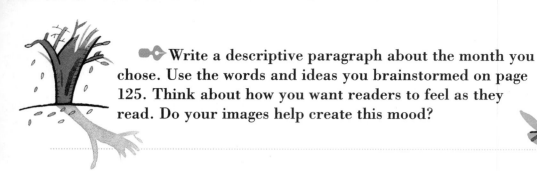

Write a descriptive paragraph about the month you chose. Use the words and ideas you brainstormed on page 125. Think about how you want readers to feel as they read. Do your images help create this mood?

126

Descriptive writing creates word pictures and feelings in the reader.

Reading Authors: Avi

Avi (a nickname from his twin sister Emily) has been writing since he was a child. Avi taught himself to write through hard work and reading: "That's what you do when you become a writer—you read a lot." He has always been fascinated by stories of adventure. The characters in his stories tend to be risk takers with powerful imaginations.

Avi's writing is fast-paced, with cliffhangers at the ends of chapters to keep readers guessing what will happen next. Predicting, Avi believes, is a vital skill. We often want immediate answers, "like in a TV sitcom," where all problems are solved in 30 minutes. Life, Avi reminds us, isn't like that.

What Next?

In *The True Confessions of Charlotte Doyle*, Avi introduces us to a young girl traveling alone by ship from England to America in the 1800s. But there is also a lot that Avi *doesn't* tell the reader. Avi is an author who likes to keep readers guessing. It's his way of encouraging readers to make **predictions**.

Asking questions about a story—and then coming up with answers to them—is an important part of predicting. As you read, jot down in the Response Notes any questions you have about Charlotte Doyle and her life. Try to write at least one prediction on each page.

Response Notes

from *The True Confessions of Charlotte Doyle* by Avi

Not every thirteen-year-old girl is accused of murder, brought to trial, and found guilty. But I was just such a girl, and my story is worth relating even if it did happen years ago. Be warned, however, this is no *Story of a Bad Boy,* no *What Katy Did.* If strong ideas and action offend you, read no more. Find another companion to share your idle hours. For my part I intend to tell the truth as *I* lived it.

But before I begin relating what happened, you must know something about me as I was in the year 1832—when these events transpired. At the time my name *was* Charlotte Doyle. And though I have kept the name, I am not—for reasons you will soon discover—the *same* Charlotte Doyle.

How shall I describe the person I once was? At the age of thirteen I was very much a girl, having not yet begun to take the shape, much less the heart, of a woman. Still, my family dressed me as a young woman, bonnet covering my beautiful hair, full skirts, high button shoes, and, you may be sure, white gloves. I certainly wanted to be a *lady.* It was not just my ambition; it was my destiny. I embraced it wholly, gladly, with not an untoward thought of anything else. In other words, I think from **The True Confessions of Charlotte Doyle** by Avi

that at the time of these events I was not anything more or less than what I appeared to be: an acceptable, ordinary girl of parents in good standing.

Though American born, I spent the years between my sixth and thirteenth birthdays in England. My father, who engaged in the manufacture of cotton goods, functioned as an agent for an American business there. But in the early spring of 1832, he received an advancement and was summoned home.

My father, an ardent believer in regularity and order, decided it would be better if I finished out my school term rather than break it off midyear. My mother—whom I never knew to disagree with him—accepted my father's decision. I would follow my parents, as well as my younger brother and sister, to our true home, which was in Providence, Rhode Island.

Lest you think that my parents' judgment was rash in allowing me to travel without them, I will show you how reasonable, even logical, their decision was.

First, they felt that by my remaining a boarder at the Barrington School for Better Girls (Miss Weed, eminent and most proper headmistress) I would lose no school time.

Second, I would be crossing the Atlantic—a trip that could last anywhere from one to two months—during the summer, when no formal education took place.

Third, I was to make my voyage upon a ship owned and operated by my father's firm.

Fourth, the captain of this ship had acquired a reputation—so my father informed me—for quick and profitable Atlantic crossings.

Then there was this: two families known to my parents had also booked passage on the ship. The adults had promised to function as my guardians. Having been told only that these families included children (three lovely girls and a charming boy) I

from **The True Confessions of Charlotte Doyle** by Avi

had looked forward to meeting them more than anything else.

So when you consider that I had but dim memories of making the crossing to England when I was six, you will understand that I saw the forthcoming voyage as all a lark. A large, beautiful boat! Jolly sailors! No school to think about! Companions of my own age!

One more point. I was given a volume of blank pages—how typical of my father!—and instructed to keep a daily journal of my voyage across the ocean so that the writing of it should prove of educational value to me. Indeed, my father warned me that not only would he read the journal and comment upon it, but he would pay particular attention to spelling—not my strongest suit.

Keeping that journal then is what enables me to relate now in perfect detail everything that transpired during that fateful voyage across the Atlantic Ocean in the summer of 1832.

JOURNAL

Choose one of the questions you wrote down in the Response Notes. In the space below, write an answer to the question. Phrase your answer in the form of a prediction about what might happen next in the story.

I predict

●⟜ Does the first line of Avi's story make you wonder why Charlotte is accused of murder? Use your imagination to invent one possible explanation. Pretend you are Charlotte Doyle and write "the truth" about what happened in your journal.

Journal of Charlotte Doyle, 1832

Asking questions is an important part of making predictions.

Conflict Between Characters

Conflict arises between characters when the wants and needs of one character clash with those of another character. Conflict causes the tension in a story to rise. As readers, we usually want to see the conflict resolved—we want things to turn out okay. When the conflict is resolved, the tension is eased, and as readers we feel a sense of relief.

Read the following passage from Avi's *The Barn*. What tension, or conflict, is there between the characters? Identify these points with a star in the Response Notes. Do you feel a release of tension at any point? If you do, circle this part.

Response Notes

from ***The Barn*** by Avi

Feeling lost, I went out to the cow and talked to her and scratched her ears. Of a sudden she turned around and butted my face. That a cow could respond more than my father made my heart swell with pain, and in my anger I struck her on her rump.

Then I rebuked myself for such thoughts and actions and once again returned to the house and took up my place by Father's bed.

His eyes had turned almost lively. He opened his mouth, and one of his strange sounds sputtered out. The spit came, too, and made his beard glisten.

I sat up and gaped at him, not certain if I was seeing something different. "Are you trying to talk?" I demanded.

When he made no further response, my momentary excitement crumpled to naught.

Frightened that I could find nothing more to tell him, I walked around the house, fetched some potatoes, and thought to cut them up. But I left them on the table and turned back to Father. I had come up with something to say.

"Nettie," I shouted at him. "Nettie told me you were planning to build a barn! A real barn to show our luck had turned!"

from **The Barn** by Avi

The moment I said that, I realized how sinful I was being, as if I were mocking him. Of course there was no reaction. Not at first. But then his mouth opened and his eyes shifted. We stared at each other for a long time. How strange his eyes seemed. They were brown, flecked with tiny spots of gold, the pupils black and enlarged to let in such light as there was.

Again I had the sense that I was looking into a cave. What was I seeing inside now?

I leaned forward. Our faces were but inches apart. "Father!" I shouted. "Nettie told me you were planning to build a barn! A real one! Is that true?"

He gazed dumbly at me.

"Father!" I shouted again. "If you *were* thinking of a barn—*close* your eyes! Close your eyes!"

There was some movement of muscle and a raspy gargle from his throat. Something twitched around his mouth, too, but those eyes remained staring wide and empty.

Suddenly all my anger rushed together within my chest. It was as if I had been struck by a musket ball. Why had he done this? It was a cruel thing he had become, and I felt a hatred for it. He had abandoned us when we needed him. He had become a child when *we* were the children. He had failed us. Oh, I so wanted to strike him and make him feel my pain.

"Father!" I screamed in annoyance. "If you mean *yes*, you *must* close your eyes!"

And then—he did.

When I realized he had given me an answer, I was so stunned I burst into tears.

━✦ How does this passage make you feel?

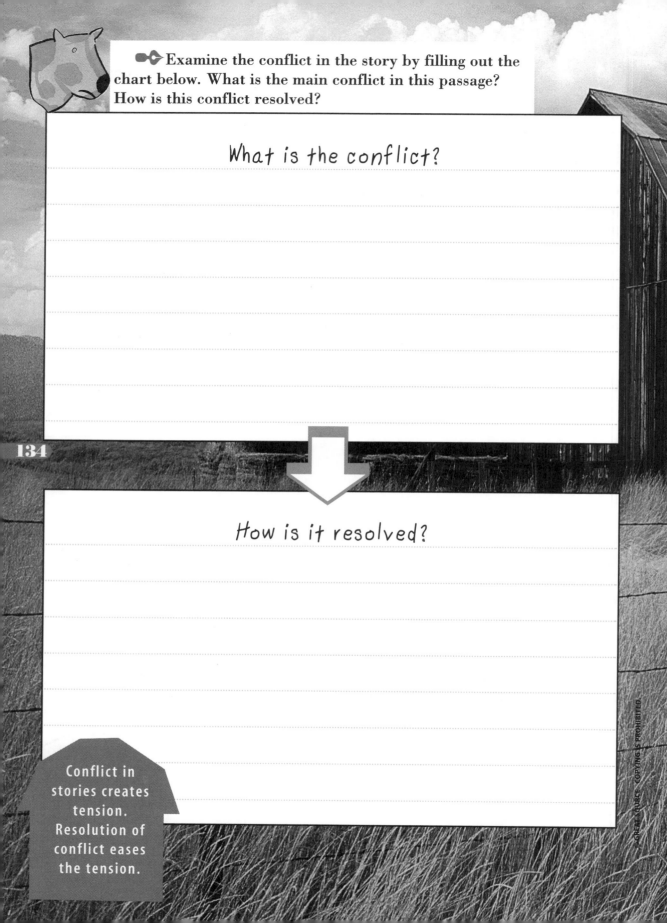

●◆ Examine the conflict in the story by filling out the chart below. What is the main conflict in this passage? How is this conflict resolved?

What is the conflict?

134

How is it resolved?

Conflict in stories creates tension. Resolution of conflict eases the tension.

Through *My* Eyes

Everyone has his or her own point of view, or way of seeing things. In a story, point of view is the angle from which the story is told. Sometimes a story is told from **first person** point of view, or through the eyes of the person living the story. Other times, it is told through **third person** point of view, or the way an onlooker might see it.

What difference does point of view make? Ask yourself that question as you continue reading *The Barn*. Is the story told from first or third person point of view? What do we learn about the narrator from this point of view? Put an X beside each moment where you feel the narrator reveals strong feelings.

Response Notes

from *The Barn* (continued) by Avi

Father had been talking about a barn before he was struck. And it was mention of a barn that allowed me to see he could understand us and give answers with his eyes. Suddenly it came to me how I might be able to stir life back into him.

I ran to the house to sit with Father again. I was dripping wet but paid no mind. He was staring straight ahead into the gloom. Gathering up my courage, I said, "Father, we need a new barn, don't we?"

He shifted and after a few moments gave the yes sign with his eyes. He tried to talk, and I could see that his fingers grew uncommon agitated.

Encouraged, I cried, "Father, that barn is *very* important to you, isn't it?"

Again, his reply was yes.

"Can you tell me how important?" I said, trying to push him on.

For a response he only gaped at me. But I would not give up. I fetched the lamp, lit it, and set it down so we could see each other clearly. Then, once again, I tried: "Father, how *important* is it to *you* that we have a *new* barn? You *must* find a way to *tell* me."

His eyes blinked some, but I wanted more.

from **The Barn** (continued) by Avi

"*Show* me how important!" I demanded. "You've got to."

He opened his mouth and made his sounds. But that was nothing new. I shook my head and cried, "I need *more*!"

He shut his eyes. His body tightened. His feet twitched. His fingers fluttered. It was like some strong man preparing to lift a huge load. In fact, what he did was jerk his right hand up. In fairness it was hardly more than an inch. But I could not have read him more plainly if he had written it out.

From that moment on, I was certain I had found the way to bring him back to life: we would build him a barn.

☞ Notice the use of the pronoun "I" in this passage: *I tried, I wanted more, I demanded.* Answer the questions below about point of view.

1. Who is telling the story?

2. Is this first person or third person point of view?

3. What do you learn about the narrator?

●◆ Reread the passage and try to see the events through the father's eyes. Write one paragraph from the father's point of view, describing what he is thinking and how he feels.

137

Point of view affects what readers learn about in a story.

Identifying Author's Style

If an author's style is crisp, clear, and to the point, he or she will probably use short sentences, simple words, and state ideas directly. If an author's style is imaginative and whimsical, he or she may use playful language and unusual words.

As you read the passage from *The Blue Heron* by Avi, jot words in the Response Notes that describe his style. Underline or highlight any moments in the text—words, expressions, images—that stand out for you.

Response Notes

from *The Blue Heron* by Avi

Maggie stepped to the marsh edge. Once there, she eased off her sneakers and stepped carefully into the water. It was almost warm. "I'm not going to hurt you," she announced. The bird lifted its head and looked at her.

Maggie took another step forward. This time she sank into the soft bottom. Almost losing her footing, she swayed precariously.

"I'm okay," Maggie said softly, and took another step forward. The bird continued to watch her. Maggie, returning the look, suddenly knew what she wanted to do, had to do. She would touch the bird. If she could touch it, all would be well, because touching the magic meant you and the magic became one.

"Would you let me?" Maggie asked, as if the bird already knew what she was thinking and could answer. But the heron only stared fixedly at her.

As Maggie began to move forward, her heart beat furiously. She had the sensation that she was moving the way the heron did, contemplating each movement, each part of each movement. Her eyes were on the bird and nothing else. She lost all sense of time. And always, she kept one hand extended before her, fingers loose, shivering gently like an undulating fan.

Gradually the distance between them decreased. The heron, as if transfixed, held its place, its eyes staring right at Maggie. Maggie could see now that

from *The Blue Heron* by Avi

the bird's colors were much more complex than she had seen from the shore. There were shades of grays, blues, blacks. Even the whites had many shades. She began to see individual feathers, how they were layered, how coarse some were, while others were fine and small. And though the bird was standing still, the tips of some feathers fanned and flowed, ruffling in a breeze that Maggie could not feel.

"Please, please," Maggie pleaded softly. "Please let me touch you."

There seemed to be no sound but the beating of her heart, no sense of motion that was movement. Instead there was an unfolding that brought her closer and closer. And as she drew nearer and nearer, the heron continued to gaze at her with its unblinking lemon eyes.

There were but twenty inches now from the tip of Maggie's fingers to the heron's crown. Every part of her body seemed to be tingling. It would take two more steps. One more step. Maggie held her breath. Then, as slowly as she had ever done anything in her life, she shifted her right foot up, heard the slight sucking sound as it pulled against the bottom mud, moved it forward even as she stretched as far as possible, her arm and fingers quivering . . . and gently—hardly more than a breath of finger to feather—she touched the heron on the side of its head and sensed the silky down of the tiny feathers, its warmth, its life.

The bird blinked and slowly coiled back its head. Then it turned and without any movement of panic or sound of alarm, rose up out of the water into the air. With its great wings flapping, it flew away.

Maggie, her heart pounding, and not knowing whether to laugh or cry, watched it go.

Response Notes

139

Look at the words, phrases, or images you highlighted in this passage. How did the parts you highlighted make you feel?

Choose one paragraph from the story and circle it. Try rewriting the paragraph in your *own* style. When you are finished, compare your paragraph to the one by Avi.

140

A writer's style affects how readers react and respond to what they read.

Reading Well

Good drivers are always watching the signs: signal lights, traffic changes, directions. Good readers do much the same thing. They watch for clues the writer gives them that can make reading easier. You can use such things as a table of contents, titles and subheads, boldface words, or (in some writing) graphs to help you pull meaning out of the text.

In the selections that follow, you'll have a chance to explore strategies that can help you make sense of what you read. You'll learn about

- skimming
- using graphics
- taking notes
- using context clues

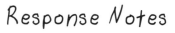

Skimming Can Tell You a Lot

Have you ever watched just the first three or four minutes of a movie and then been able to guess what the movie was going to be about? Movies—and good writing—are full of clues. You do not have to read an entire book or article to get a sense of what is coming.

Running your eyes quickly over the page—a strategy known as **skimming**—can help you predict what the selection will be about. Try it. Instead of reading the whole passage from *Top of the World* word for word, skim it. Read the title and the first paragraph. Then let your eyes move quickly down the page. Pay attention to boldface headings. As you go, circle four or five words that seem to give a sense of what this article is about.

Response Notes

from *Top of the World* by Steve Jenkins

Mount Everest is a place of great beauty, adventure, and danger. If you ever want to climb it, here are a few things to think about.

Up and Down

At 29,000 feet, there is only one third as much oxygen as at sea level. In fact, if someone at sea level were suddenly transported to the top of Everest, he or she would die within a few minutes from the lack of oxygen. To prepare for the extremely thin air, you must make several round trips from base camp to higher and higher points on the mountain, sometimes spending the night before starting back down. Staying for increasing periods of time high on the mountain helps keep you from getting altitude sickness.

Avalanche!

When snowfall builds up on a steep mountainside, a whole section of a slope may break loose suddenly and slide down the mountain, moving at speeds of up to 200 miles per hour. More climbers on Mount Everest are killed by avalanches than by anything else.

Hold On

Mount Everest is so tall that it's affected by the jet stream, a narrow, fast-moving air current that

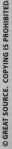

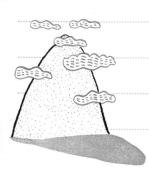

from *Top of the World* by Steve Jenkins

circles the world six to ten miles above sea level.

High winds on the mountain make climbing—and surviving—much more difficult. Blowing snow can make it difficult to see, and wind-chill makes the low temperatures feel even colder. The winds are so strong at times that climbers have actually been blown right off the mountain.

Brrr!

The constant cold adds to the challenge of high-altitude mountain climbing. At the top of Everest, typical high temperatures in summer are around −20°F. Nighttime temperatures of −100°F are common. To make matters worse, when there's less oxygen available, it's much harder to stay warm. Well-insulated clothes are a matter of life or death on the mountain.

The Death Zone

Above 26,000 feet, there is so little oxygen that climbers' bodies can't adapt. Anyone who remains at this elevation will get weaker and weaker and eventually die. That's why, once they reach this altitude, climbers have to get to the summit within a day or two. If they don't, they must descend to a lower camp.

The Summit

When you stand on top of Mount Everest, you are the highest thing on earth. For most people, reaching this point is the reward for years of hard work and planning. You can't stay long, though. Your body needs oxygen, which means getting back to a lower altitude quickly. Because you're so exhausted, the descent is one of the most dangerous parts of the climb, so you'll have to be very careful on the way down.

143

➡️ Now, using what you know just from skimming, predict what you think will be the main points of this article. Don't worry about being right—just use the clues your eyes grabbed with a quick sneak peek to make some good guesses.

This article is probably about

Plus

And maybe

Or

➡️ Now go back and read the article to check out your predictions. Then rate yourself as a skimmer on this 1 to 4 scale.

1.	2.	3.	4.
I need to look more closely!	I guessed right on a point or two!	I picked up over half the points just by skimming!	I got almost the whole message!

When you skim, glance through a selection quickly and track down key points.

Take Time for Graphics

It's amazing how many people think reading means simply focusing on words. Actually, reading is much more than this. Good readers take in the whole picture: they notice charts, graphs, photographs, maps, and illustrations. They also pay special attention to words in big or bold type. They use every ounce of information an author provides to draw meaning from a text.

As you read the following passage from "The Spirit of Reform," pay attention to the *whole text*. Underline, circle, or star information you think is important. Then ask yourself, "Was that what the author most wanted me to notice?"

"The Spirit of Reform" from *We the People*

Across western New York, people gathered at huge outdoor revival meetings to hear the fiery words of minister Charles Finney. With piercing eyes and shaking fists, Finney boomed a simple message: work hard, go to church, don't drink alcohol, and help others live useful lives. Finney was part of a religious movement that swept the United States in the early 1800s. The Second Great Awakening, as it was called, inspired many Americans to join volunteer groups and get involved with social concerns.

The Antislavery Movement

One of the most important reform movements during the time of the Second Great Awakening was the antislavery movement. Since the 1700s, free African Americans like Philadelphia businessman James Forten had worked hard to abolish, or end, slavery. People who fought against slavery came to be known as **abolitionists.**

In 1829, an African American named David Walker wrote four articles, known today as his *Appeal.* "Freedom is your natural right," he told enslaved people. During the 1830s, the antislavery

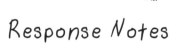

Response Notes

"The Spirit of Reform" from *We the People*

movement grew. Leading the way was a white
Massachusetts man named William Lloyd Garrison.
In speeches and articles, Garrison spoke out
harshly against slavery. In 1833, he and other
leading abolitionists founded the American
Anti-Slavery Society.

146

Response Notes

"The Spirit of Reform" from *We the People*

In 1841, Frederick Douglass heard Garrison speak. Douglass, who had only recently escaped from slavery, soon became an influential leader in the antislavery movement:

> **"My acquaintance with the movement increased my hope for the ultimate freedom of my race, and I united with it from a sense of delight, as well as duty."**

Other abolitionists, both black and white, helped African Americans to escape from slavery. They worked on a system called the Underground Railroad. The **Underground Railroad** didn't have a locomotive or tracks, and it didn't run underground. It was a secret network of men and women, called "conductors," who led enslaved workers to freedom. Men, women, and children were moved from one safe house, called a "station," to the next. *(See map on the previous page.)*

147

➥As you read "The Spirit of Reform," what kinds of things did you highlight, circle, or star? Check each one you marked.

_____ Names of people or places or concepts

_____ Dates

_____ Words in bold print

_____ Quotations (words actually spoken by people)

_____ Map

_____ Other:

➥Look again at the map that goes with this article. What does the map teach you that you would not learn from the text alone?

Suppose *you* were the publisher of "The Spirit of Reform." In addition to the map, what kinds of graphics would you want to include? (Remember: a graphic should help explain or extend the information in the text.)

In the space below, describe four additional graphics to go with this article. They could be photographs, timelines, charts, graphs, or anything else you think would be helpful. Place a number in the Response Notes to show where each graphic would go.

THE SPIRIT OF REFORM

148

Graphic 1	Graphic 2

Graphic 3	Graphic 4

Graphics help readers understand and visualize information

Note Taking: An Art

There's a trick to taking good notes. The best note takers seem drawn like human magnets to the most important ideas. They never write down *everything*. When an author writes, "More than 230 species of sharks inhabit the oceans of the world," a good note taker writes simply "Sharks—230 species." Get the idea?

As you read this passage on electrons by Bill Nye, take notes. Try not to write *everything*. Focus only on the important points.

from *Bill Nye the Science Guy* by Bill Nye

Electrons are way out away from the nucleus, and they go zipping around it—all day, all the time. Electrons have a **negative electric charge** (–), so they're attracted to the positively-charged protons. "Opposites attract."

When scientists first figured out that electrons exist, they assumed that the electrons were in orbit around the nucleus, just like the Moon is in orbit around the Earth. Later scientists discovered it's a little more complicated than that: electrons move around in strange, untraceable patterns. We know they're more likely to be in some places than others, but we never know exactly where. The electrons' patterns are called **"orbitals"** [OAR-bit-alls]. For many experiments you can still think of electrons as whirling in orbit, though.

Electrons are much smaller than protons and neutrons. It takes about 1800 electrons to weigh as much as one proton, and that proton is mighty tiny to begin with. Also, electrons are zipping around very fast. As a result, electrons quite often can be jolted off of atoms and go hang out somewhere else.

Here's one astounding fact about atoms. If an electron were the size of a basketball, the nucleus

Response Notes

Response Notes

from *Bill Nye the Science Guy* by Bill Nye

would be the size of a car. And, even weirder, the basketball would be almost 30 kilometers away. That's right, 20 miles! Think about that. It means that atoms are mostly empty space. And everything made of atoms (like you and me) is also mostly empty space. Just space. Nothing.

150

➥ What is the most interesting thing you learned from this article? Why is it interesting to you?

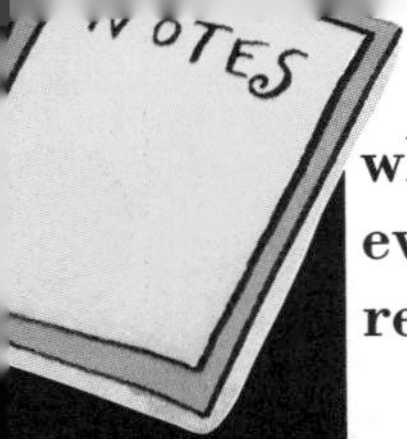

NOTES

It's easier to write good notes if you think about why we do it. Mostly, it's because we cannot remember everything we hear or read. No one can. Notes are reminders.

Use your notes to summarize the main idea and three other things you learned from the article.

Summary (using only my notes!)

Main Idea

Three Details

1.

2.

3.

Taking notes is one good way to remember the most important ideas from

As a reader, you may sometimes find yourself face to face with words you don't know. Often, the meaning of a word can be found right there in the text you are reading. When you use the words or sentences around an unfamiliar word in order to figure out its meaning, you are using **context clues**.

As you read, picture yourself using a mental magnifying glass to uncover the word clues the author has given you. Guess what each underlined word might mean. Write your guesses in the Response Notes. Also highlight context clues—the words or phrases that give you the best hints about each word's meaning.

Response Notes

from *Matilda* by Roald Dahl

It is bad enough when parents treat *ordinary* children as though they were scabs and bunions, but it becomes somehow a lot worse when the child in question is extraordinary, and by that I mean sensitive and brilliant. Matilda was both of these things, but above all she was brilliant. Her mind was so **nimble** and she was so quick to learn that her ability should have been obvious even to the most half-witted of parents. But Mr. and Mrs. Wormwood were both so **gormless** and so wrapped up in their own silly little lives that they failed to notice anything unusual about their daughter. To tell the truth, I doubt they would have noticed had she crawled into the house with a broken leg.

Matilda's brother Michael was a perfectly normal boy, but the sister, as I said, was something to make your eyes pop. By the age of *one and a half* her speech was perfect and she knew as many words as most grown-ups. The parents, instead of applauding her, called her a noisy chatterbox and told her sharply that small girls should be seen and not heard.

from **Matilda** by Roald Dahl

By the time she was *three*, Matilda had taught herself to read by studying newspapers and magazines that lay around the house. At the age of *four*, she could read fast and well and she naturally began **hankering** after books. The only book in the whole of this enlightened household was something called *Easy Cooking* belonging to her mother, and when she had read this from cover to cover and had learnt all the recipes by heart, she decided she wanted something more interesting.

Response Notes

●◆ Create a word web for each underlined word. In each web, write the words or phrases that give you clues about the word's meaning.

153

nimble

gormless

hankering

●✦ Use your webs to guess the meaning of each underlined word. Write your guess in the first column. Then use a dictionary to check your guess against the actual definition.

	My Guess	Dictionary Definition
nimble		
gormless		
hankering		

●✦ Look through the dictionary to find a word you don't know. Read the definition. Now, write a short paragraph in which you make the word's meaning clear. Provide hints about the word's meaning in your paragraph, but don't define it.

Context clues can help you discover the meaning of words you don't know.

SOAP BOX

Reading About Issues

When you are reading about issues, it's especially important to be an active reader. In order to understand and form an opinion about issues when reading, ask yourself these questions:

1. Is the author using facts or opinions, or both?

2. Does the author have a position, or bias, on the issue?

3. Is the author presenting both sides of an issue?

4. What is the author's tone, or attitude, toward the issue?

In this unit, you will have the chance to read about several issues. Think about the opinions, bias, and tone in each selection. As you read, notice how each piece makes you feel and whether the writing influences you to change your *own* opinions.

Facts vs. Opinions

Writers of nonfiction often use a mix of facts and opinions. As a reader, you need to be able to sort these out. A fact is something that can be proved. If you did research, you could find out whether it was true or false. An opinion, on the other hand, is someone's personal idea. An opinion cannot be proven true or false. You may agree with an opinion, of course, and *believe* it to be true. The big difference is that you cannot *prove* it is true.

Read *There Was a Time* by James Haskins. As you read, underline or highlight three or four statements of fact. Put a letter "F" in the Response Notes beside them. Also underline or highlight three or four statements of opinion. Put a letter "O" in the Response Notes beside them.

Response Notes

There Was a Time by James Haskins

Many of the laws that governed life in the South were laws of segregation—separating the races. Throughout Southern cities there were signs that read White and Colored. These signs designated separate facilities for each race: public drinking fountains and restrooms, bus station entrances and the buses themselves, movie theaters and sports arenas.

The races were separated in other ways by custom. Black people were expected to call white people Mr. and Mrs. and Miss, while white people called black people by their first names. Blacks were supposed to step aside when whites passed by. A black person could be arrested for talking back to, or "sassing," a white person.

This time in the American South was not the time of slavery. It was one hundred years after slavery had ended. But blacks were still not free.

Life for blacks in the North was better than in the South, but Northern blacks lived under difficult conditions too. They did not have to live under the Southern system of legal segregation. But they

There Was a Time by James Haskins

suffered from discrimination that kept them from getting good jobs and having equal opportunities with whites.

Since the end of slavery, black people in both the North and the South had often tried to win their civil rights, or full rights of citizenship, and real freedom. In 1892 Homer Plessy brought suit against the Louisiana railroad company that forced him to sit in a segregated car. His case went all the way to the United States Supreme Court, which ruled in 1896 in *Plessy v. Ferguson* that segregation was constitutional as long as "separate but equal" facilities were provided to blacks and whites.

In 1917 ten thousand blacks marched down Fifth Avenue in New York City to protest racial discrimination. In the 1920s Chicago blacks staged a "Jobs-For-Negroes" campaign. In 1936 the National Association for the Advancement of Colored People (NAACP) began to bring suit in Southern courts for equal pay for black teachers.

In the 1940s the Congress of Racial Equality (CORE) staged sit-in demonstrations for integration at a Chicago restaurant and tested segregation policies on interstate bus lines. Blacks in New York demonstrated for and won the right to be hired at white-owned Harlem businesses and local utility companies. Mass meetings were held to protest discrimination in the national defense effort during World War II.

Blacks had sometimes won small gains, but they still did not enjoy the basic rights of citizenship that white people took for granted. In a democracy like the United States, the majority rules, and whites are in the majority. Blacks even today are only eleven percent of the population. In order for blacks to gain their civil rights, they had to make most whites believe they were entitled to them.

That is what the civil rights movement of the 1950s and '60s hoped to accomplish. By demanding

There Was a Time by James Haskins

their rights through peaceful protest, but not resorting to violence when whites tried to break up their demonstrations, blacks challenged the conscience of white America. They forced whites to see them as human beings just like themselves and to see that their cause was right.

The March on Washington was a high point in the civil rights movement. It was the largest demonstration for human rights in the history of the United States. It was also the largest demonstration that had ever occurred in the nation's capital. Other events had drawn more spectators than the estimated 250,000 people who attended that historic event on Wednesday, August 28, 1963, but no other event had attracted as many actual participants.

The march was also the largest peaceful demonstration in Washington, D.C., to date. In the day-long event just three arrests were made. Not only was it a peaceful march, it was an integrated march. Of the quarter of a million marchers, as many as 60,000 were white.

But it was primarily a black march, and it had been the idea of a black man. That made it another first. The March on Washington was the largest organized Negro political event that had ever been supported by the white power structure. In this case, the power structure was the President and Congress of the United States.

Look carefully at the parts you highlighted and any notes you made. Based on your own responses, how would you describe Haskins's article?

___ Mostly opinions

___ Mostly facts

___ About the same number of opinions and facts

Writers support their opinions with facts. Find one or two facts to support each of these opinions.

Blacks were still not free.

1.

2.

The March on Washington was a high point in the civil rights movement.

1.

2.

Is there a topic—for example, homework or allowance—that you have strong feelings about? Brainstorm both facts and opinions about your topic.

Topic:

Facts	Opinions

Use your brainstorming notes to write a paragraph
about your topic. Use a combination of fact and opinion
in your paragraph to tell how you feel and why you feel
the way you do.

Topic:

Beware of Bias

It's easy to let **bias**—a tendency to favor one opinion over another—slip into our writing. As a reader, it is important to be on the lookout for bias. For example, a writer may cite more support for one side of an issue than the other. Or some arguments could be presented more convincingly than others. Some writers go so far as to leave important evidence out of their writing altogether!

Read "Loch Ness" once. Decide what side of this issue the author seems to lean toward. Then go back and jot down in the Response Notes any words, sentences, or bits of evidence that show the author's bias.

"Loch Ness" by Patricia Thomas

Sunlight dances down the blue expanse of Loch Ness. A light breeze stirs the water where Castle Urquhart guards the curve of the bay. It is a fine, calm day to launch a boat or cast a line. Or is it?

Is something out there? An upturned boat? A log? A mass of water plants? Or could it be Nessie—the fabled Loch Ness Monster?

For centuries, debate has raged over whether a huge, unknown creature inhabits this mysterious loch—largest, longest, and deepest of three lakes threading Scotland's wildly beautiful Great Glen.

Vikings may have been first to ask the question. Their mythology tells of "water horses" in Scotland's lochs. The first *written* account of a lake creature dates back to the sixth century when, says an ancient Latin text, a swimmer was killed by a frightful beast near the loch's north end. St. Columba, on hearing of the attack, rowed out and scolded the monster so severely that never since has it been known to repeat such a misdeed.

Rumors and whisperings of a "horrible great beastie" continued, century after century. But they were spoken in hushed tones and not often when strangers were about. In the 1930s, however, word

Response Notes

"Loch Ness" by Patricia Thomas

of the Loch Ness Monster began to spread. Nessie made a big splash in 1934 when Rupert Gould, a respected scientific writer, published a book called *The Loch Ness Monster and Others.*

Residents and visitors to the loch began coming forward with stories of sightings, some from earlier times. An elderly gentleman wrote to Gould, recalling that about 1871 he saw something "like an upturned boat . . . wriggling and churning up the water." In a startling land encounter, a London couple driving home from a holiday in 1933 saw an enormous, black "prehistoric animal" loom in front of them, then shuffle into the loch.

Stories grew more dramatic, descriptions more specific. The classic image of Nessie with long neck, multiple humps, and long tail emerged.

The first photo of Nessie was snapped by a workman who watched "an object of considerable dimensions" rise out of the dark loch. His photo is believed to be authentic, but it is too blurry to prove anything. A clearer (but, as it turned out, much less authentic) shot of Nessie labeled "the surgeon's picture" was produced by Robert Wilson, a London doctor. Although years later the photo was proven to be a hoax, it remains the best known likeness of Nessie.

Hoaxes (and, possibly, hallucinations) aside, the case for a real Nessie continued to grow. Researchers began using modern tools to find an answer to the riddle. In the 1970s, a team of scientists used sonar to track two objects, 20 to 30 feet long, and photographed them with an underwater camera. A photo showed what looked like a big flipper with a bulky, rough-textured body.

Although debate still rages, emphasis seems to have shifted from trying to prove whether Nessie exists to determining what she could be. **Cryptozoologists** suggest it might be a primitive snakelike whale called a *zeuglondon,* a long-necked seal, or a school of giant eels. Prevailing opinion,

162

"Loch Ness" by Patricia Thomas

Response Notes

however, favors the idea that Nessie is a plesiosaur, a descendant of dinosaurs long thought extinct but somehow able to survive in the deep loch. Undoubtedly, of course, Nessie is not alone. To have survived for so many centuries, she must be part of a breeding family. In fact, more than one creature has been seen at once—though such sightings are rare.

The mystery is far from solved. No one theory fits all data. Scientists even argue about what is actually "data." No body or body parts identified with the monster have ever been found. And ancient myth may be, after all, simply myth.

But some photos and films do appear to be authentic. Reported Nessie sightings now number more than 3,000—and counting.

Arthurian legend tells of Sir Lancelot's quest to the north, where he slew a great water dragon. Perhaps there is more truth to those old tales than we imagine after all.

163

🖋 What do you think the author believes about Nessie? Give examples from the text to explain your answer.

Do you have a lot of opinions? Do you like to present your side of things? Here's your chance. Pick a topic you have strong opinions about, and write a totally biased essay on your topic. Don't even consider the other side.

My important topic is ....

Totally Biased Essay

164

Writing that is biased favors one side of an issue over another.

Presenting Both Sides

Every issue has at least two sides. When you read informational writing, ask youself how well the author has presented both sides of the issue. If you feel only one side has had its fair say, you may want more information before you make up your mind.

In "Schools Crack Down on Peanuts," the author examines both sides of an issue. As you read, put a plus sign (+) beside passages that seem to *support* the crackdown; put a minus sign (–) beside passages that seem to be *against* the crackdown. When you finish reading, ask yourself, "Does the author lean toward one side (*for* the crackdown) or the other (*against* the crackdown)? Or does the writer do a good job of balancing both sides?"

Response Notes

"Schools Crack Down on Peanuts"

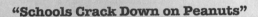

Sheri Davis opens her bag and pulls out a peanut butter sandwich. She hears the harsh voice of the lunch lady behind her. "Freeze! Put down the sandwich and move slowly away from the table!"

It's not quite that bad yet, but administrators are getting serious about keeping peanuts and peanut products out of schools. Why? Some kids are so severely allergic to peanuts that contact with even a speck of a peanut can mean death. To protect students with such allergies, schools across the country have banned peanut products from their campuses.

School officials say that the bans are a sensible way to protect allergic students. Opponents of bans say they punish non-allergic students unfairly.

The Deadly Peanut

According to the Food Allergy Network (FAN), a group that promotes knowledge of food allergies, between 1 million and 2 million Americans have peanut allergies. Peanut allergies are more serious than most allergies. In extreme cases, they can

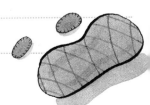

result in death by causing a sudden drop in blood pressure and closing the breathing passages. The FAN says that 125 people in the United States die from food allergies each year, many from peanut allergies. The Centers for Disease Control and Prevention (CDC), however, places the number at about six deaths a year. Regardless of the figures, peanut bans in schools, say supporters, can save lives.

For saving those lives and protecting the health of millions of others, the inconvenience of school peanut bans is a small price to pay, ban supporters add. That was the thinking at Lomarena Elementary School in Laguna Hills, Calif., where they have instituted a voluntary peanut ban. Principal Sharon Vestermark explained, "It has in many cases been an inconvenience for the other parents, but we have to put the life of [a] child first."

Bans Are Nuts

Many people, however, think banning peanuts is unfair. Forbidding a nutritious and inexpensive food like peanuts is unfair to the majority of kids who do not have allergies, say ban opponents.

"We don't want people who are allergic to eat peanuts, but . . . we have to respect the 99.5 percent of the population who want [peanuts]," said Mitch Head, executive director of the Peanut Advisory Board.

Opponents argue that bans are unrealistic and unworkable anyway. Many unbanned foods, such as cereals and candy bars, can contain small but dangerous traces of peanuts.

Some ban opponents suggest setting up peanut-free zones in school cafeterias. Some schools use these zones already. Other people say that people with allergies should take the responsibility of avoiding dangerous foods.

How do you think schools should handle the peanut problem? Why?

Look back at the passages you marked with a plus or minus. Notice the language used. List some of the words or phrases here.

Words that seem to **support** the ban on peanuts ...

Words that seem **against** the ban on peanuts ...

167

Based on your reading of the article, do you think the author fairly presented the two sides? Explain.

Now that you have read "Schools Crack Down on Peanuts," where do you stand? Write a letter to your school paper expressing your opinion. Be sure to tell why you feel as you do. Use evidence from the article or from your experience.

168

When you read about issues, ask yourself whether the author has presented both sides.

4 A Persuasive Tone

It isn't always what a writer says that makes us agree or disagree with the message in a piece of writing. Often, it's the *way* in which he or she says it. The writer's **tone** is the attitude the writer takes toward the subject. The tone of a message may touch our feelings so strongly that we find ourselves going along with what the writer has to say—whether the argument is a strong one or not. Good readers try to be aware of what is influencing their thinking: Is it facts and ideas? Or is it the writer's voice and tone?

Read *Galápagos* by Ann McGovern. Underline or highlight any lines or words where you feel the writer's tone comes through clearly. In the Response Notes, jot down any emotions or feelings the tone brings out in you.

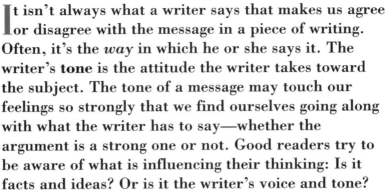

Response Notes

Galápagos by Ann McGovern

Day Two. Santa Cruz

Dear Diary,
This morning we anchored in Academy Bay off Santa Cruz, one of the four islands in the Galápagos where people live.

I'm so excited! After lunch I'm going to see giant Galápagos tortoises—the largest land tortoises in the world! At the Charles Darwin Research Station I'll get to see them up really close. Grandma says the station was named for Charles Darwin, who sailed to the Galápagos in 1835 on the ship the *Beagle* and later became a famous scientist.

I just found out that *galápagos* means tortoise in old Spanish.

Later

Dear Diary,
I am so mad I could cry!
I read up on giant tortoises before lunch. Once there were hundreds of thousands of these huge tortoises on the Galápagos Islands.

Response Notes

Galápagos by Ann McGovern

Long ago, explorers, pirates, and seal and whale hunters came here. They stayed at sea for many months, and sometimes years. The fresh meat of the giant tortoises kept them from starving to death. The sailors knew that tortoises can stay alive for a year without food or water, so they stacked them by the hundreds in the damp, dark holds of their ships, one on top of another. Oh, those poor creatures.

Rats are no friends of tortoises, either. There were never rats here until the ships brought them. The rats swam to shore and began to destroy tortoise eggs and young tortoises. Rats are still around today. No wonder there are so few giant tortoises left.

The good news is that today there's hope for the tortoises. Andy told me that thanks to the Charles Darwin Research Station and the National Park Service, a lot of giant tortoises are being saved.

➥ Look at the first "Dear Diary" entry. What is the tone of this passage? Circle any words that you think describe the tone at the beginning.

Angry	Excited	Sad	Happy
Serious	Scared	Humorous	

Other:

■━○ Now look at the second "Dear Diary" entry. What is the tone of this passage? Circle any words that you think describe the tone. Did the tone change?

Angry   Excited   Sad   Happy

Serious   Scared   Humorous

Other:

■━○ In the first column of the chart, write the words you chose to describe the tone of the diary entries. In the second column, jot down examples—words or phrases from the text—that show the tone.

Tone	Example from Diary
Example: Happy, excited	"I'm so excited!"

How do you feel about the tortoises of the Galápagos Islands after reading McGovern's diary entries? Describe your own feelings below.

How much do you think the tone of the diary entries influenced your opinion?

☐ Not one bit

☐ Some

☐ A lot

A writer's tone can affect the way readers feel about a topic.

Understanding Language

Sometimes big gifts come in small packages—like poems, for instance. Poets pack a lot of punch into the fewest words necessary. They choose words carefully to convey feelings and insights in a unique way.

Each poem you read offers a unique experience. A poem may make you laugh, surprise you with a startling image, or share an insight into life. In this unit, you'll read poems that do each of these things.

To get the most out of poems you read in this unit, you'll use active reading strategies such as visualizing, highlighting, and asking questions. You'll explore the craft of poetry and reflect on your own personal responses to the poetry you read.

Experiencing a Poem

A poem isn't meant just to be understood—it's meant to be experienced. Think of yourself as a sponge, soaking up all a poem has to offer. To do this, read the poem out loud, so that you can listen to the way the words flow. As you listen, picture in your mind what the words describe.

When you read a poem, explore your responses to it by asking and answering questions like these:

- How does the poem make me feel?
- What does it make me think about?
- What feelings or experiences of my own does the poem remind me of?

Read the following poem aloud. Then ask yourself the questions above and jot down your responses in the Response Notes.

Response Notes

A Little Girl's Poem by Gwendolyn Brooks

Life is for me and is shining!
Inside me I
feel stars and sun and bells singing.

There are children in the world
all around me and beyond me—
here, and beyond the big waters;
here, and in countries peculiar to me
but not peculiar to themselves.

I want the children to live and to laugh.
I want them to sit with their mothers and fathers
and have happy cocoa together.

I do not want
fire screaming up to the sky.
I do not want
families killed in their doorways.

Life is for us, for the children.

A Little Girl's Poem by Gwendolyn Brooks

Life is for mothers and fathers,
life is for the tall girls and boys
in the high school on Henderson Street,
is for the people in Afrikan tents,
the people in English cathedrals,
the people in Indian courtyards;
the people in cottages all over the world.

Life is for us, and is shining.
We have a right to sing.

➤ In the space below, draw a picture that, for you, captures the feeling of this poem.
- What things do you see?
- What colors do you see?
- Whom do you see? Where are they?

175

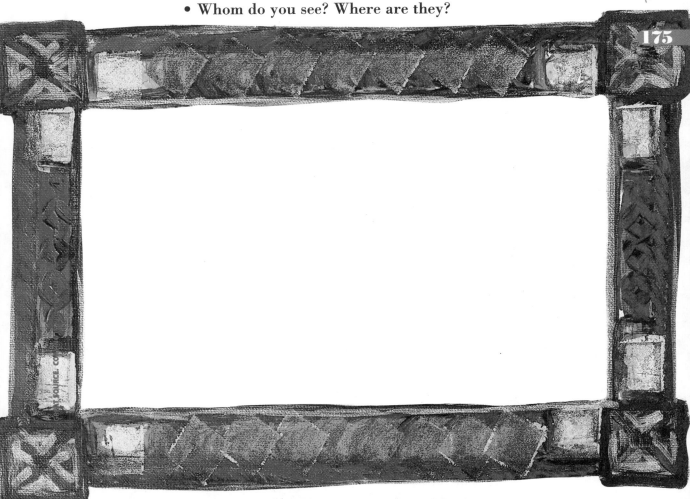

The speaker in this poem is a little girl. Compare how the little girl in the poem feels about life to how you feel.

How the little girl in the poem feels	How I feel about life

176

When you read poetry, reflect on what it makes you think about and feel.

2 Giving Human Traits

When writers give human qualities to something that is not human, it's called **personification**. Personification is a way to make ordinary objects come to life. In "Winter Poem," Nikki Giovanni uses personification to express a strong feeling. First read the poem aloud and listen to the sound of the words. Then read it again, this time stopping to check your understanding of the poem. In the Response Notes, jot down answers to the following questions:
- What is the poet personifying?
- What human qualities has the poet given to this non-human thing?

Winter Poem by Nikki Giovanni

Response Notes

once a snowflake fell

on my brow and i loved

it so much and i kissed

it and it was happy and called its cousins

and brothers and a web

of snow engulfed me then

i reached to love them all

and i squeezed them and they became

a spring rain and i stood perfectly

still and was a flower

⬤◣ What feeling about snow is the poet expressing in this poem?

◗◆ Nikki Giovanni makes snow come alive by using personification in her poem. Select one of the following experiences from nature that you would like to explore in a poem.

Cool Breeze   Warm Sunshine

Soft Rain   Thunder and Lightning

Other: ....

Now brainstorm thoughts, ideas, and feelings about the topic you chose. Write the topic you chose in the web. Then add words and phrases that make the topic come alive.

Use your brainstorming ideas to write a poem. Try including examples of personification to express your feelings about your topic and to bring it to life.

179

Poets use personification to express feelings and bring ordinary objects and experiences to life.

Striking Images

Many poets use **imagery**—words that paint mental pictures—to convey a feeling in their poems. Visualizing is a reading strategy that will help you experience the imagery in a poem. When you visualize, you picture in your mind what the words describe. Try to visualize this sentence:

> *The lone boy shuffled through the rubbish in the empty lot, half-heartedly kicking along a rusted tin can.*

What feeling do you get from the words?

As you read "The Rider," try to visualize the imagery. Put a star by the lines that create pictures in your mind. In the Response Notes, describe the feelings that you get from the imagery.

180

Response Notes

The Rider by Naomi Shihab Nye

A boy told me
if he rollerskated fast enough
his loneliness couldn't catch up to him,

the best reason I ever heard
for trying to be a champion.

What I wonder tonight
pedaling hard down King William Street
is if it translates to bicycles.

Response Notes

The Rider by Naomi Shihab Nye

A victory! To leave your loneliness
panting behind you on some street corner
while you float free into a cloud of sudden azaleas,
luminous pink petals that have never felt loneliness,
no matter how slowly they fell.

In the space below, sketch what you visualized
when you read the last stanza (last five lines) of the poem.

Picture a scene from your own life in your mind. It could be a scene from school, home, or outdoors. Describe the scene in a paragraph. Be sure to include imagery—specific words and details—that help the reader picture what you're describing.

182

When you encounter imagery in a poem, picture in your mind what the words describe.

The Sound of a Poem

Just as songs have a beat, so do poems. The beat, or pattern of sound in a poem, is called **rhythm.** Many poems, like some songs, also have **rhyme,** or words that end in similar sounds. The rhyming words often occur at the ends of the lines in a poem. Rhythm and rhyme add to the pleasure of reading a poem and can help the poet convey a specific feeling.

In the poem "Jimmy Jet and His TV Set," poet Shel Silverstein uses a regular rhythm and pattern of rhyme. Read the poem aloud to hear the sound of the words. Then go back and highlight the words that rhyme. Read the poem again and tap out its rhythm.

Jimmy Jet and His TV Set by Shel Silverstein

I'll tell you the story of Jimmy Jet—
And you know what I tell you is true.
He loved to watch his TV set
Almost as much as you.

He watched all day, he watched all night
Till he grew pale and lean,
From "The Early Show" to "The Late Late Show"
And all the shows between.

Response Notes

Jimmy Jet and His TV Set by Shel Silverstein

He watched till his eyes were frozen wide,
And his bottom grew into his chair.
And his chin turned into a tuning dial,
And antennae grew out of his hair.

And his brains turned into TV tubes,
And his face to a TV screen.
And two knobs saying "VERT." and "HORIZ."
Grew where his ears had been.

And he grew a plug that looked like a tail
So we plugged in little Jim.
And now instead of him watching TV
We all sit around and watch him.

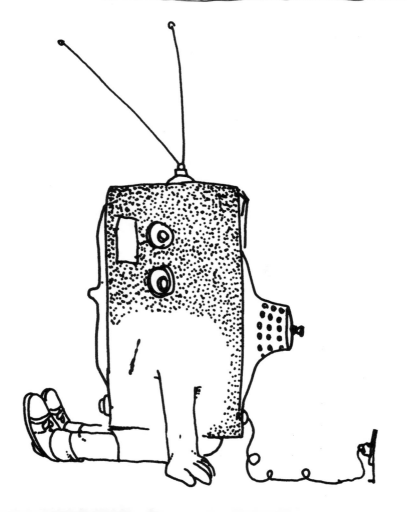

⬤➤ **What kind of feeling do you get from this poem?**

⬤➤ **Answer each question below.**

1. What line rhymes with:
   "I'll tell you the story of Jimmy Jet—"?

185

2. What line rhymes with the last line:
   "We all sit around and watch him"?

3. Make up some lines of your own that have the same rhythm and rhyme as the poem you read.

I'll tell you the story of _____

And you know what I tell you is _____

Continue writing the poem you began on the previous page. Try to imitate the pattern of rhythm and rhyme in Shel Silverstein's poem.

Rhythm and rhyme contribute to the feeling that you get from a poem.

Reading Authors: Betsy Byars

I often think of my books as scrapbooks of my life, because I put in them all the neat things that I see and read and hear. I sometimes wonder what people who don't write do with all their good stuff.
—Betsy Byars

Betsy Byars has found enough "good stuff" in her life to create more than fifty books, including one that won a Newbery Medal. In her writing, Byars draws not only upon her own life experiences but also upon incidents and people she has read or heard about. In discussing her writing, Byars rates characters as the number one element in a story. "The characters are the key to the story," she says. You'll see this emphasis on characterization in the works you read in this unit.

Predicting a Character's Reactions

An author can use a number of methods to show readers what a character is like. These methods, called **characterization**, include:

- directly stating the character's traits
- describing the character's appearance
- showing how the character acts and talks
- revealing the character's thoughts and feelings

When an author successfully develops a character, readers feel like they understand that character. In fact, readers may understand a character so well that they can predict how the character will react.

Now read a passage from *The Pinballs*. Pay attention to the way Byars characterizes Carlie on the first page. Then use this information to try to predict how Carlie will react to her new foster mother. Write your prediction in the Response Notes.

Response Notes

Your prediction:

from *The Pinballs* by Betsy Byars

Carlie had been suspicious of people since the day she was born. She swore she could remember being dropped on the floor by the doctor who delivered her.

"You weren't dropped," her mother had told her.

"All right then, why is my face so flat? Was I *ironed*?"

Carlie also claimed that when she was two months old a baby-sitter had stolen a golden cross from around her neck.

"No baby-sitter stole a gold cross from you," her mother had told her.

"All right then, where is it?"

Carlie believed everyone was out to do her in, and she had disliked Mrs. Mason, the foster mother, as soon as she had seen her standing in the doorway.

"I knew she'd have on an apron," Carlie said to the social worker. "She's trying to copy herself after Mrs. Walton—unsuccessfully, I might add."

from **The Pinballs** by Betsy Byars

"Maybe she has on the apron because she was cooking, Carlie."

"*I* should be the social worker. I'm not fooled by things like aprons."

She also didn't like the Masons' living room. "This is right out of 'Leave It to Beaver,'" she said. She especially distrusted the row of photographs over the fireplace. Seventeen pictures of—Carlie guessed—seventeen foster children.

"Well, my picture's not going up there," she grumbled to herself. "And nobody better snap me when I'm not looking either." She sat.

Mrs. Mason waited until "Young and Restless" was over and then she said, "Carlie?"

"I'm still here."

"Well, come on and have some lunch. Then afterward you can help me get the boys' room ready."

Carlie turned. She looked interested for the first time. "The boys?" she asked. "There're going to be some boys here?"

"Yes, two boys are coming this afternoon—Thomas J and Harvey."

"How old?"

"Eight and thirteen."

"Oh, boo, too young." Carlie got up from the footstool. "What's wrong with them?"

"Wrong with them?"

"Yeah, why do they have to be here? I'm here because I got a bum stepfather. What's their trouble?"

"Well, I guess they'll have to tell you that."

Carlie lifted her hair up off her neck. "How about the thirteen-year-old?" she asked. "What's he like? Big for his age, I hope."

"He has two broken legs. That's about all I can tell you."

"Well," Carlie said, "that lets out dancing."

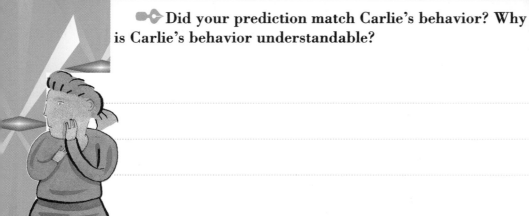

■●◆ Did your prediction match Carlie's behavior? Why is Carlie's behavior understandable?

....

....

....

■●◆ What methods does Byars use to develop the character of Carlie? Find one example from the story for each method of character development described below.

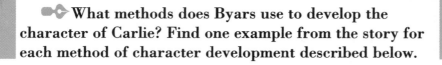

Method	Example from story
directly states the character's traits	
describes the character's appearance	
shows how the character acts and talks	
reveals the character's thoughts and feelings	

◖━◆ Knowing that Carlie is suspicious of people, it's easy to understand her behavior. Think of a character trait, such as kind, shy, or sneaky. Then write a character sketch about someone who has that trait. Begin by describing the trait. Then show how the character behaves in a way that demonstrates this trait.

191

Based on an author's character-ization, a reader can sometimes predict how a character will react.

2

The Role of Minor Characters

Sometimes minor characters play an important role in stories. They not only add interest to the stories but also help reveal information about the main characters.

The following passage comes from *The Cybil War*, a story about two friends who like the same girl. As you read, pay attention to Byars's characterization of the minor character Pap-pap. Note what you learn about the main character Simon by the way he reacts to Pap-pap. Underline any sentences and phrases that give you clues about how Simon feels about his father.

Response Notes

from *The Cybil War* by Betsy Byars

Simon and Tony were known as best friends. Their friendship had been sealed in second grade when the entire class was asked to write essays on their fathers.

Simon refused to write one, and Tony could not because his father had died when he was one year old. Tony could not even remember his father. So they had sat at their desks, both miserable, both staring at their dirty fingernails, while other children went to the front of the room and read happily, "My father is a dentist. He plays golf. He plays tennis. He has a new car."

When the voting was held on the best paper—Billy Bonfili won because his father was the high school football coach—only Simon and Tony did not vote.

"You don't have a father?" Tony asked after school. He had waited at the door to ask this, his long face intent.

"I have one," Simon said carefully, "but he's gone."

"Where?"

"I don't know."

from ***The Cybil War*** by Betsy Byars

"I had one but he's dead."

"Oh."

And thus sealed together by a mutual loss rather than mutual interest, their friendship had begun. They walked together to Tony's house.

"You like ravioli?" Tony asked at the edge of the walkway.

"I don't know."

"You never had ravioli?"

"No."

"Well, come *on!*"

They went into Tony's house, and Simon sat at the kitchen table. He watched while Tony heated the ravioli. He was looking down at his steaming plate, at the strange, soft squares, when Tony's grandfather came in.

"You want some ravioli, Pap-pap?" Tony asked at the stove.

Pap-pap nodded, pulled out his chair, sat heavily. When the three of them were seated, plates full, Tony said, "He doesn't have a father either."

Pap-pap looked over at Simon. His eyes, blue as a baby's, began to fill with tears. "You got no papa?"

"I have one but he's gone."

Pap-pap pulled out his handkerchief. It was old and faded because it was used all the time. "Your papa left home?" he asked.

"Yes."

"He comes to visit?"

"No."

"He writes?"

"We got one letter."

"One letter," Pap-pap said sadly. He shook his head. Tears spilled onto his wrinkled cheeks. He wiped his eyes and blew his nose.

"He cries a lot," Tony explained to Simon.

Simon nodded. He looked from Tony to the weeping Pap-pap. Simon had not seen his mother cry when his father left. He himself had not cried.

from *The Cybil War* by Betsy Byars

And here, across the table, from an old man he had never seen before, were tears for his father. He felt the first stirring of tears in his own eyes.

"Sometimes he cries just because the moon's full, you know, because it's beautiful," Tony explained, as he chewed. "And sometimes he cries because he sees a picture that reminds him of home, and sometimes—well, he just cries all the time. It doesn't mean anything."

Simon nodded again.

"That's not true," Pap-pap said. "It means something." He peered at them over his handkerchief. "It means I get so full I spill over." He made a gesture with his handkerchief as if it were water pouring over a dam. Then he wiped his cheeks again and, sniffling, began to eat.

Simon ducked his head, cut a piece of ravioli in half with his fork and put it in his mouth. The tears in his own eyes, the tightening of his throat made him unable to swallow, but there was something in the soft warm food, the weeping sympathetic man across the table that would make him feel sentimental every time he ate ravioli. Even in the school cafeteria, where ravioli came straight from a can, he would feel tears in his eyes when he ate.

What do you learn about Simon through Pap-pap?

Imagine that you are Simon. Write a journal entry describing how you feel about Tony and his grandfather, Pap-pap.

195

Sometimes minor characters help reveal information about a main character.

3

Who's Telling the Story?

The **point of view**, or angle from which a story is told, affects the information an author presents. A first-person point of view means that one of the characters is telling the story. The narrator uses the pronoun *I*. A third-person point of view means that someone outside the story is telling it. The narrator describes events using the pronouns *he*, *she*, and *they*. A first-person narrator cannot tell the thoughts of other characters, while a third-person narrator can.

   The Summer of the Swans is a story about a teenager and her mentally retarded brother, Charlie. As you read, underline pronouns that indicate the point of view. Then identify the point of view in the Response Notes.

Response Notes

from *The Summer of the Swans* by Betsy Byars

Charlie awoke, but he lay for a moment without opening his eyes. He did not remember where he was, but he had a certain dread of seeing it.

There were great parts of his life that were lost to Charlie, blank spaces that he could never fill in. He would find himself in a strange place and not know how he had got there. Like the time Sara had been hit in the nose with a baseball at the Dairy Queen, and the blood and the sight of Sara kneeling on the ground in helpless pain had frightened him so much that he had turned and run without direction, in a frenzy, dashing headlong up the street, blind to cars and people.

By chance Mr. Weicek had seen him, put him in the car, and driven him home, and Aunt Willie had put him to bed, but later he remembered none of this. He had only awakened in bed and looked at the crumpled bit of ice-cream cone still clenched in his hand and wondered about it.

His whole life had been built on a strict routine, and as long as this routine was kept up, he felt safe and well. The same foods, the same bed, the same furniture in the same place, the same seat on

from *The Summer of the Swans* by Betsy Byars

the school bus, the same class procedure were all important to him. But always there could be the unexpected, the dreadful surprise that would topple his carefully constructed life in an instant.

The first thing he became aware of was the twigs pressing into his face, and he put his hand under his cheek. Still he did not open his eyes. Pictures began to drift into his mind; he saw Aunt Willie's cigar box which was filled with old jewelry and buttons and knickknacks, and he found that he could remember every item in that box—the string of white beads without a clasp, the old earrings, the tiny book with souvenir fold-out pictures of New York, the plastic decorations from cakes, the turtle made of sea shells. Every item was so real that he opened his eyes and was surprised to see, instead of the glittering contents of the box, the dull and unfamiliar forest.

He raised his head and immediately felt the aching of his body. Slowly he sat up and looked down at his hands. His fingernails were black with earth, two of them broken below the quick, and he got up slowly and sat on the log behind him and inspected his fingers more closely.

Then he sat up straight. His hands dropped to his lap. His head cocked to the side like a bird listening. Slowly he straightened until he was standing. At his side his fingers twitched at the empty air as if to grasp something.

He took a step forward, still with his head to the side. He remained absolutely still.

Then he began to cry out in a hoarse excited voice, again and again, screaming now, because he had just heard someone far away calling his name.

To see how much difference point of view makes, rewrite this passage from Charlie's point of view. Use the pronoun *I*. Be sure to include only what Charlie knows, thinks, feels, or experiences.

The point of view determines what information is presented and how it is presented in a story.

A Sense of Humor

Authors sometimes use humor to soften painful situations. In her stories, Byars helps readers see the humor in the struggles that many young people face.

One way of creating humor is by exaggerating, or overstating the truth. Notice how Byars uses exaggeration for its humorous effect in this passage from *Bingo Brown, Gypsy Lover*. As you read, try to visualize what is going on. In the Response Notes, draw sketches of your mental pictures.

from *Bingo Brown, Gypsy Lover* by Betsy Byars

His arms were growing! They had grown about four inches since this morning! They were sticking out of his jacket sleeves!

He stepped back in alarm. He glanced down at himself. Nothing else about him was growing—just his arms. He looked like a scarecrow!

He bent to examine his legs to see if by some miracle they had grown too. But his pants weren't too short, just his jacket sleeves.

He looked from one arm to the other. How had he not noticed that this terrible thing was happening?

He glanced around quickly to see if any shoppers were aware of his distress. They weren't, and Bingo drew his arms back into his sleeves to make them less noticeable. He pulled the cuffs over his wrists.

They still stuck out!

When had this happened? Were his arms continuing to grow even as he stood here? By the time he got home would his knuckles be dragging on the ground like an ape?

A voice behind him said shyly, "Hi, Bingo."

He spun around, and immediately realized he could never spin around again. His arms were like weapons. The girl was lucky she hadn't been whirled into the bookshelves.

Response Notes

199

from **Bingo Brown, Gypsy Lover** by Betsy Byars

She said again, "Hi."

It was a girl from school—a new girl, but even if she had been his oldest and dearest friend Bingo would not have been able to remember her name at this crucial moment.

"You just bumped into me—didn't you notice—back at the toy store?"

"No, no, but I'm sorry."

"Oh, you already said that," she smiled, "—back at the toy store."

"Oh."

"You looking for a book?" she asked.

"I was . . . I don't know. . . . You'll have to excuse me—I just had a terrible shock."

"What kind of shock?"

"Personal," Bingo said. "It was a personal shock."

"Most of them are."

Bingo clutched the cuffs of his jacket with his fingers and stretched them down. The bones of his wrists were still—as he knew they would be—exposed.

"I thought when I saw you standing over here in romances, that maybe you were buying your mom's Christmas present because, I don't know, you don't seem the type to be reading this kind of book. I would have expected to find you back in something like—" A pause for emphasis. "—science fiction."

He was unable to speak.

"If that's what you were doing," she went on helpfully, apparently unaware of the growth that was occurring inside his sleeves.

And his arms were growing. He could feel it happening at this very moment! The bones were elongating and the flesh and muscles were going right along, stretching like rubber bands—

"If that's what you were doing—shopping for your mom, I could recommend *Wild Reckless Summer*—this one." She touched the picture of a

from **Bingo Brown, Gypsy Lover** by Betsy Byars

woman with a lot of hair on her head being embraced by a pirate with a lot of hair on his chest. "There's *Wild Reckless Autumn* and *Wild Reckless Winter* and *Wild Reckless Spring*, but my sister says *Wild Reckless Summer* is the best."

At the moment, Bingo was so worried about wild reckless growth that he had no idea what she was babbling about. She might as well have been speaking in Hindu.

Go back over the passage. Highlight the parts that you find humorous. Choose your favorite part and draw a cartoon below that shows what is happening to Bingo. Add a caption beneath the cartoon.

What would you say to Bingo Brown if you met him in person? What advice would you give him? If you want, make your advice to Bingo as humorous as his story.

Authors sometimes use exaggeration to create humor in a story.

8 "The Three-Century Woman" by Richard Peck. Reprinted by permission of Richard Peck.

18 "Little Hare and the Pine Tree" by Joseph Bruchac. Reprinted by permission of Joseph Bruchac.

23 Excerpt from *Princess in the Pigpen.* Copyright © 1989 by Jane Resh Thomas. Reprinted by permission of Houghton Mifflin Company. All rights reserved.

27 From *Mistakes that Worked* by Charlotte Foltz Jones. Illustrations by John O'Brian.

30 "About Loving" from *Hey World, Here I Am!* by Jean Little. Copyright © 1986 by Jean Little.

34 "The Wonderful Emerald City of Oz" from *The Wizard of Oz* by Frank Baum. Copyright © 1958 by TAB Books. Reprinted by permission of Scholastic Inc.

37 From *There's a Boy in the Girls' Bathroom* by Louis Sachar. Copyright © 1987 by Louis Sachar. Reprinted by permission of Alfred A. Knopf Children's Books, a division of Random House, Inc.

41 "The Birds' Peace" by Jean Craighead George. Copyright © 1990 by Jean Craighead George.

48 From *In the Year of the Boar and Jackie Robinson* by Bette Bao Lord. Copyright © 1984 by Bette Bao Lord.

52 "The Sidewalk Racer" from THE SIDEWALK RACER AND OTHER POEMS OF SPORT AND MOTION by Lillian Morrison. Copyright © 1965, 1967, 1969, 1977 by Lillian Morrison. Used by permission of Marian Reiner for the author.

55 "Desert Tortoise" by Byrd Baylor. Reprinted with the permission of Atheneum Books for Young Readers, an imprint of Simon & Schuster Children's Publishing Division from DESERT VOICES by Byrd Baylor. Text copyright © 1981 Byrd Baylor.

59 From *Silverwing* by Kenneth Oppel. Reprinted with the permission of Simon & Schuster Books for Young Readers, an imprint of Simon & Schuster Children's Publishing Division. Text copyright © 1997 Kenneth Oppel.

64, 67 From *Beetles, Lightly Toasted* by Phyllis Reynolds Naylor. Reprinted with the permission of Atheneum Books for Young Readers, an imprint of Simon & Schuster Children's Publishing Division. Copyright © 1987 Phyllis Reynolds Naylor.

70 From *Boys Against Girls* by Phyllis Reynolds Naylor. Reprinted with the permission of Atheneum Books for Young Readers, an imprint of Simon & Schuster Children's Publishing Division. Copyright © 1994 Phyllis Reynolds Naylor.

74 From *Shiloh* by Phyllis Reynolds Naylor. Reprinted with the permission of Atheneum Books for Young Readers, an imprint of Simon & Schuster Children's Publishing Division. Copyright © 1991 Phyllis Reynolds Naylor.

80 From *Orphan Train Rider: One Boy's True Story* by Andrea Warren. Copyright © 1996 by Andrea Warren. Reprinted by permission of Houghton Mifflin Company. All Rights Reserved.

82 Excerpt from *The Snake Scientist* by Sy Montgomery. Text copyright © 1999 by Sy Montgomery. Photographs copyright © 1999 by Nic Bishop. Reprinted by permission of Houghton Mifflin Company. All rights reserved.

87 From *The Tarantula* by Gail LaBonte © 1990. Reprinted by permission of Prentice-Hall, Inc., Upper Saddle River, NJ.

90 From *Under Our Skin: Kids Talk About Race.* Text copyright © 1997 by Debbie Holsclaw Birdseye and Tom Birdseye. All rights reserved. Reprinted by permission of Holiday House, Inc.

96, 99 Excerpt from *Lincoln: A Photobiography* by Russell Freedman. Copyright © 1987 by Russell Freedman. Reprinted by permission of Clarion Books/Houghton Mifflin Company. All rights reserved.

103 Excerpt from *A River Ran Wild,* copyright © 1992 by Lynne Cherry, reprinted by permission of Harcourt, Inc.

108 "At-mun" from *Amos Fortune, Free Man* by Elizabeth Yates. Copyright © 1950 by Elizabeth Yates McGreal, renewed © 1978 by Elizabeth Yates McGreal. Used by permission of Dutton Children's Books, a division of Penguin Putnam Inc.

114 From *My Life as a Fifth-Grade Comedian* by Elizabeth Levy. Copyright © 1997 by Elizabeth Levy.

118, 120 "Spaghetti" from *Every Living Thing* by Cynthia Rylant. Reprinted with the permission of Simon & Schuster Books for Young Readers, an imprint of Simon & Schuster Children's Publishing Division. Copyright © 1985 Cynthia Rylant.

123 Prologue from *Tuck Everlasting* by Natalie Babbitt. Copyright © 1975 by Natalie Babbitt. Reprinted by permission of Farrar, Straus and Giroux, LLC.

128 From *The True Confessions of Charlotte Doyle* by Avi. Copyright © 1990 by Avi. Reprinted by permission of Orchard Books, New York. All rights reserved.

132, 135 From *The Barn* by Avi. Copyright © 1994 by Avi. Reprinted by permission of Orchard Books, New York. All rights reserved.

138 From *The Blue Heron* by Avi. Reprinted with the permission of Simon & Schuster Books for Young Readers, an imprint of Simon & Schuster Children's Publishing Division. Copyright © 1992 by Avi Wortis.

142 "Top of the World" from *Top of the World: Climbing Mount Everest* by Steve Jenkins. Copyright © 1999 by Steve Jenkins.

145 "The Spirit of Reform" from WE THE PEOPLE by Hartoonian, et al. Copyright © 1997 by Houghton Mifflin Company. Reprinted by permission of Houghton Mifflin Company. All Rights Reserved.

149 From *Bill Nye the Science Guy's Big Blast of Science* by William Nye. Copyright © 1983 by William Nye and TVBooks, Inc. Reprinted by permission of Perseus Books Publishers, a member of Perseus Books, L.I.C.

152 From *Matilda* by Roald Dahl. Copyright © 1988 by Roald Dahl. Used by permission of Puffin Books, a division of Penguin Putnam Inc.

156 "There Was a Time" from *The March on Washington* by James Haskins. Copyright © 1993 by James Haskins.

161 "Loch Ness" by Patricia Thomas, from *Faces: People, Places, and Cultures*, January 2000. Copyright © Cobblestone Publishing Company.

165 "Schools Crack Down on Peanuts" from *Weekly Reader.* Special permission granted, 'Current Events' published and copyrighted 1998 by Weekly Reader Corporation. All rights reserved.

169 "Adventures in the Galápagos" from *Swimming with Sea Lions* by Ann McGovern. Copyright © 1992 by Ann McGovern. Reprinted by permission of Scholastic Inc.

174 "A Little Girl's Poem" by Gwendolyn Brooks, from *Very Young Poets*, copyright © 1983 by The David Company.

177 "Winter Poem" from *My House* by Nikki Giovanni. Copyright © 1972 by Nikki Giovanni. Reprinted by permission of HarperCollins Publishers, Inc.

180 "The Rider" by Naomi Shihab Nye. Used by permissions of Naomi Shihab Nye.

183 "Jimmy Jet and His TV Set" from *Where the Sidewalk Ends* by Shel Silverstein. Copyright © 1981 Evil Eye Music, Inc. Used by permission of HarperCollins Publishers.

188 From *The Pinballs* by Betsy Byars. Copyright © 1977 by Betsy Byars.

192 From *The Cybil War* by Betsy Byars. Copyright © 1981 by Betsy Byars. Used by permission of Viking Penguin, a division of Penguin Putnam Inc.

196 From *The Summer of the Swans* by Betsy Byars. Copyright © 1970 by Betsy Byars. Used by permission of Viking Penguin, a division of Penguin Putnam Inc.

199 From *Bingo Brown, Gypsy Lover* by Betsy Byars. Copyright © 1990 by Betsy Byars. Used by permission of Viking Penguin, a division of Penguin Putnam Inc.

Book Design: Christine Ronan and Sean O'Neill, Ronan Design

Cover Photographs: Ostrich, © Kevin Horan/Stone; Landscape, © Daryl Benson/Masterfile

Illustrations on pages 7, 17, 33, 47, 63, 79, 95, 113, 127, 141, 155, 173, and 187, © Lisa Adams. Illustrations on pages 183 and 184, © Shel Silverstein. All other illustrations © Leslie Cober-Gentry.

Photo Research and **Text Permissions:** Feldman and Associates

Developed by Nieman Inc.

The editors have made every effort to trace the ownership of all copyrighted selections found in this book and to make full acknowledgement for their use. Omissions brought to our attention will be corrected in a subsequent edition.

author's purpose, the reason why an author writes.

autobiography, a true story written by a person about his or her own life.

bias, favoring or presenting only one side of an argument.

biography, a true story written by one person about another person's life.

brainstorm, jotting down thoughts about a subject in order to get ideas for writing.

cause and effect, a relationship in which one event or action (the cause) makes another event or action (the effect) happen.

character, a person, animal, or imaginary creature in a story.

compare and contrast, examining the ways in which two or more things are alike and different.

conflict, the problem in a story.

context clues, using the words and sentences around an unknown word to figure out the word's meaning.

details, in nonfiction, facts and examples that are used to support the main idea. In fiction, words and description that add interest to writing.

description, writing that uses details to paint a picture of a person, a place, a thing, or an idea.

dialogue, talking between characters in a story.

draw conclusions, using prior knowledge and information in the text to gain a deeper understanding of a piece of writing.

exaggeration, a description that stretches the truth. Exaggeration is used in tall tales.

fact, a statement that can be checked or proven to be true.

fantasy, a story that includes imaginary characters or happenings that are not realistic.

fiction, writing that tells an imaginary story.

figurative language, using words in a special way in order to create a picture in the reader's mind. (See, for example, *simile*, *metaphor*, and *personification*.)

first-person point of view, a story told by one of the characters, using the pronoun *I*.

folktale, a story that is passed down orally from one generation to the next.

graphic aid, a picture that helps readers understand facts, ideas, and information. Graphic aids include graphs, charts, maps, and diagrams.

highlight, a way to mark the information during reading that is most important or that you want to remember.

imagery, words and details that create mental pictures in the reader's mind.

206

inferences, using details from reading and what you already know to understand what you read.

journal, a written record of thoughts, feelings, and ideas.

main idea, the most important point in a piece of writing.

metaphor, a comparison that does not use the word *like* or *as.*

narrative nonfiction, writing that combines elements of fiction (for example, dialogue) with elements of nonfiction (for example, historical names and dates).

nonfiction, writing about real people, places, things, or ideas.

note-taking, writing down only the most important ideas from what you read.

onomatopoeia, words that sound like their meanings, such as *thump* and *hiss.*

opinion, a view or belief held by a person.

paragraph, a group of sentences that tell about one subject or idea.

personification, a figure of speech in which an idea, object, or animal is given human qualities.

persuasion, writing that is meant to change the way readers think or act.

plot, the action of a story.

poetry, a special kind of writing in which words are chosen and arranged to create a certain effect.

point of view, the angle from which a story is told.

predict, using what you already know and story clues to guess what will happen next.

prior knowledge, using what you already know to understand what you read.

realistic fiction, a story that seems as if it could be real although it is not true.

resolution, the part of the story's plot in which a problem or problems are solved.

rhyme, repeated sounds at the ends of words.

rhythm, the beat in spoken language or in writing.

sensory details, words and examples that help the reader see, feel, smell, taste, and hear a subject.

sequence, the order in which events happen.

setting, the time and place of the story.

simile, a comparison that uses the word *like* or *as.*

skim and scan, looking over a piece of writing without reading every word in order to find information quickly.

style, an author's choice of words, phrases, and sentences.

summarize, writing or telling only the most important ideas from something you have read.

synonym, a word that means about the same thing as another word.

tall tales, stories that use humor and exaggeration to tell about extraordinary heroes and heroines.

theme, the message or point of a piece of writing.

third-person point of view, a story told by someone outside the story, using pronouns *he* and *she.*

tone, an author's attitude toward a subject. A writer's tone could be serious, humorous, or angry, for example.

207

topic, the subject of a piece of writing.

topic sentence, the sentence that contains the main idea of a paragraph.

visualize, to see or picture in your mind what you read.

208